South Carolina

You Came Here to Die, Didn't You

Registering Black Voters One Soul at a Time
SOUTH CAROLINA, 1965

Sherie Holbrook Labedis

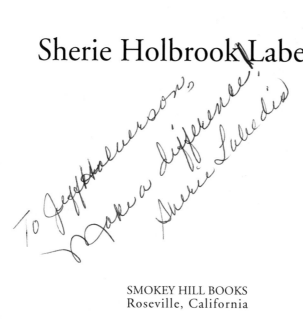

SMOKEY HILL BOOKS
Roseville, California

Labedis, Sherie Holbrook.

You came here to die, didn't you : registering black voters one soul at a time: South Carolina, 1965 / Sherie Holbrook Labedis. — Roseville, Calif. : Smokey Hill Books, c2011.

p. ; cm.

Includes index and bibliography.

ISBN: 978-0-615-42370-8

1. Civil rights—United States. 2. Civil rights—South Carolina. 3. African Americans—Civil rights. 4. African Americans—Suffrage. 5. Civil rights workers—United States. 6. Civil rights workers—South Carolina. I. Registering black voters one soul at a time: South Carolina, 1965

E185.615 .L33 2011   2010917516

323.1196073—dc22   1101

Printed in the United States of America

Cover and interior design by www.tothepointsolutions.com

*To my parents, Lois and Ralph Holbrook,
who encouraged me to be myself.*

*To my teacher, Bruce Harvey,
who guided my search for who I wanted to be.*

*To my friend Eleanor Wolf, who convinced me that others would want to
know about the summer of 1965 and its impact on who I am.*

"And so, my fellow Americans, ask not what your country can do for you; ask what you can do for your country."

President John F. Kennedy
Inaugural Address, Friday, January 20, 1961

"If a man hasn't discovered something that he will die for, he isn't fit to live."

Dr. Martin Luther King, Jr.
Speech in Detroit, Michigan, June 23, 1963

"At times history and fate meet at a single time in a single place to shape a turning point in man's unending search for freedom. So it was at Lexington and Concord. So it was a century ago at Appomattox. So it was last week in Selma, Alabama. There is no Negro problem. There is no southern problem. There is no northern problem. There is only an American problem. Many of the issues of civil rights are very complex and most difficult. But about this there can and should be no argument. Every American citizen must have the right to vote . . . Yet the harsh fact is that in many places in this country men and women are kept from voting simply because they are Negroes . . . No law that we now have on the books . . . can insure the right to vote when local officials are determined to deny it . . . There is no Constitutional issue here. The command of the Constitution is plain. There is no moral issue. It is wrong—deadly wrong—to deny any of your fellow Americans the right to vote in this country. There is no issue of States' rights or National rights. There is only the struggle for human rights."

President Lyndon B. Johnson
Speech to Congress, March 15, 1965

CONTENTS

Introduction   *xiii*

In The Beginning   1

A Lesson In Etiquette   14

Waiting On The Lord   17

Aha, So That's How It Feels   26

The Roadblock   29

A Visit From The Klan   36

What If I Fail?   39

I Have a Dream: Alienation   44

Pennies From Heaven   47

We Don't Go By That Law Down Here: Arrested   50

I Have A Dream: Newcomer   51

Hogshead Stew   56

We Don't Go By That Law Down Here: The Trial   60

Pass The Bedpan, Please   67

Contents

The Problem With Hormones   70

A Line In The Sand: Canvassing   77

A Line In The Sand: Registration Day   81

The Problem With Hormones: Problem Solved   84

In God's Hands   86

We Don't Serve Colored Here: Test   92

Go Away So Nobody Knows   95

So Much For The Hippocratic Oath   99

Fireball In The Night   103

On The Outside Thinking In   107

A Line In The Sand: Promise   110

Riding The Wave   112

We Don't Serve Colored People Here: Politics   117

Between Two Worlds   120

Looking Back   126

Epilogue   130

Acknowledgments   137

Appendix A: Pineville Freedom House
Staff and Local Workers   141

Appendix B: People   143

Contents

Appendix C: The Art of Nourishment   151

Appendix D: SCLC Orientation   153

Appendix E: SCLC Evaluation   163

Appendix F: SCLC Reading List   165

Appendix G: Resolution Passed at the Death of
Mrs. Martha Ann Middleton Prioleau Simmons   167

Appendix H: The Right to Vote   171

Bibliography   175

Credits   179

About The Author   181

Index   183

INTRODUCTION

"What are you willing to die for?" Bruce Harvey, my high school junior English teacher asked the class as he closed Thoreau's essay "On Civil Disobedience." My body trembled and I knew I wouldn't rest until I found the answer. Once found, I'd have to act.

When I was interviewed about this book in 2007, Ron Herd II of Black Talk Radio asked why I went south. My short answer was that there was a genuine need. Why didn't everyone go? But, of course, there's a much longer answer.

Writing this book made me really examine my own motivations for the first time and I discuss my feelings at length in these pages. Basically, I guess, my inspiration came from television. My parents, younger brother and I ate dinner each night on TV trays watching the national news. I found the news reports and video footage of racial incidents—such as using cattle prods to subdue young people demonstrating for the right to vote—an abomination in a country guided by our Constitution. The lessons of each evening were reiterated the next day in school by my English teacher Bruce Harvey, who reminded us that if we expected a better world, we had to fight for it.

It was too late when my parents, who had only recently gained a toehold on the middle class, realized their error; they'd taught me to make moral decisions. Other than limiting my popularity with boys, "morals" might have led to nothing more dangerous than returning library books on time or never telling a lie. Bruce Harvey introduced the idea of standing up for what I believed in. My parents unknowingly added moral responsibility and obligation. The television set the stage. The combination was too powerful to refuse.

My parents were delighted that the University of California, Berkeley, accepted their daughter in 1964. Between their pride and my swelled head, we didn't grasp that the campus simmered in protest. Free Speech, Filthy Speech, pro-Vietnam War, anti-Vietnam War, student rights and feminism. I'd been sheltered in rural California and the anti-ROTC, anti-House Un-American Activities Committee and Hands-Off-Cuba rallies were baffling to me. In fact, there seemed to be hundreds of rallies and Berkeley was divided to the right and the left as students urged one another to take a stand. If my parents had known, would they have allowed me to attend Berkeley?

The consequences of protests were clear when the National Guard, city, county and state police patrolled the entrances to the campus and arrested students. This was not protest from afar as on the television screen. Protest was suddenly in my face. Astonished, I waded through masses of protestors and my eyes watered in classes from tear gas. Fear. Confusion. Challenge. Despite all that, I felt these students were living their beliefs. Their passion intensified my personal quest and the trembling became a constant friend.

The events of the Selma-to-Montgomery March[1] in the spring of 1965 riveted my attention on the Civil Rights Movement and focused my

---

1. "Angered by the February 1965 shooting death of young black man Jimmie Lee Jackson and ready to claim their voting rights, black people in Selma [Alabama] wanted to take their anger straight to Governor Wallace in Montgomery . . . On Sunday, March 7, 600 people lined up at Brown Chapel African Methodist Episcopal Church in Selma for the fifty-mile walk to Montgomery. Their journey would be known as 'Bloody Sunday.'

"The police who lined the route did not deter the marchers. As they marched across Edmund Pettus Bridge that linked Selma to Montgomery, the scene changed dramatically. A swarm of Alabama state troopers appeared dressed in riot gear. Some were mounted on horses. Major John Cloud issued the demonstrators a two-minute warning to turn around and go back to the church. He waited, then gave the order for the state troopers to advance. Demonstrators panicked as troopers attacked. Many were overcome by tear gas, others beaten with clubs. Marchers fled for fear of being trampled by horses. Men, women and children were slugged. Sixteen marchers ended up in the hospital, another fifty received emergency treatment. Reporters covering the march caught the brutality on camera." Thomas, Velma passion. Dr. Martin Luther King, Jr.'s words resonated in my head and heart, "History will have to record that the greatest tragedy of this period of social transition was not the strident clamor of the bad people, but the appalling silence of the good people." My focus: black voter registration in the Deep South. I had never met a black person. I'd never been south of Los Angeles. A "different" culture meant a Chinese or Mexican restaurant. Thoreau wrote about accepting the consequences for one's actions. I was willing to accept the consequences, but I had no idea what they would be. My visions of sit-ins, marches, protests and freedom songs now included black students. But I had never seen true poverty. I had never smelled death. I had never heard the strangled language and drained hope of illiteracy. I had never felt smothered by prejudice. I naively believed the right to vote would bring equality.

At the same moment in Pineville, Berkeley County, South Carolina, there were black people who lived a segregated, second-class life. They wanted "freedom now," although other members of the same community feared retribution from local whites. When I arrived with three other white volunteers, many in the white community were infuriated. The stage was set and a voter registration project got a wobbly start. The other workers and I faced poverty, death, illiteracy, prejudice, the Ku Klux Klan and our preconceived ideas of people of another race.

This book is based on a journal I kept during the summer of 1965 when I, an eighteen-year-old white girl, and a group of black teenagers dared to challenge society. I've talked with other volunteers who don't remember much of what I've written. I doubt if I could remember if I didn't have my journal and pictures to prompt me. I can't guarantee dates are exact. Sometimes I didn't have time to write for several days and so much was happening, it was hard to remember it all. The "facts" are based on journal entries and my memories, although I may not always remember events and experiences exactly as they were.

My journal helped me recall individual workers but readers may find some difficulty in keeping them straight. Some tips: Workers from California are white. Workers from Pineville and the local area are black. You

---

Maia, *We Shall Not Be Moved: The Passage from the Great Migration to the Million Man March*. (New York: Crown Publishers, Inc., 2002) 20-21.

Pineville must have been a small place. According to a woman at the Information Resources and Dissemination Branch of the U.S. Census Bureau, "I have been unable to locate Pineville in any of our census years." U.S. Census Bureau 2010.

may also be confused by the ever-changing personnel. I know I was at the time. Civil rights workers, black and white, came and left the Pineville Freedom House all the time. Some stayed for a day, others for a week. The only constants in the voter registration project were the white volunteers from California: Florence, John, Nellie and me. Carol, who had ridden south to Atlanta with Ray, Julie and me, was in Pineville half the summer. Just about the time we'd get to know someone, they'd be on their way to another project.

To make things a bit easier, I have included the actual list of volunteers beginning on page 141.

And, another comment to make the book more readable: GeeChee or Gullah[2], the language of the sea islands off the coast of South Carolina and Georgia, had a strong influence on the language of the black people of Berkeley County. Gullah is a patois combining the language West African slaves brought with them and the English they found here. My first instinct was to write the local Pineville dialogue in GeeChee, because the barrier of language was one of my challenges that summer, and I thought I could convey the difficulty that came with imploring people to act in a language they didn't understand.

I didn't, of course, master it. But, I had a Gullah accent when I returned to California and no one could understand what I was saying. The first expression I learned in Pineville was "Say what?" And I used it all the time. Basically it's "pardon me." In my case it meant would you please say that again? And again? And again until I can understand?

Trying to portray the accent phonetically, however, would lead to strange spellings and omissions and be difficult to read. For example, "Mus tek cyear a de root fa heal de tree," might be an accurate representation of the voice, but it would be a struggle to read. (It means: "You need to take care of the root to heal the tree.")

However, I wanted to include the flavor of their Creole dialect. Therefore, I have used a few Gullah-based constructions. Words like "best" and "must" sounded like "bess" and "muss," so I've chosen to use "bes'" and "mus'" to indicate that I've dropped the "t." I do the same with some words ending in "d."

---

2. "The Language of the Sea Islands." Gullah Heritage: the Language of the Sea Islands. 4 Aug. 2010. <http://www.islandpacket.com/man/gullah/language.html>.

In 2008, Phil Hutchings, the last Student Nonviolent Coordinating Committee (SNCC)[3] president, commented that working on civil rights was like a roller coaster ride. "All I could do," he said, "was hold on for my life."

What caused white students to leave acclaimed universities for a dangerous roller coaster ride? Answering this question would take another book. Looking back, I realize we didn't talk often about why we came south other than that we felt needed. I don't think the why made a difference. Our commitment was all that mattered, and it was overpowering. Our time was spent learning what to do and trying to do it. I know I felt like a bit of a missionary. I felt "called" to go. I think I assumed others felt called as well.

I do know why some of the others were there. Nellie was a white student at Stanford University. While I was writing this book I contacted her and asked what had motivated her. She said that her sister was one of her reasons for joining Summer Community Organization and Political Education (SCOPE).[4] Her sister attended Spelman College, a historically black school in Atlanta, Georgia, for two years and had participated in civil rights activities while there. Raised in a liberal Mennonite family and tradition, Nellie said, "The Mennonite stand for pacifism, justice and civil rights. These are things I believe in and certainly helped influence

---

3. "In early 1960, four black students from North Carolina Agricultural and Technical College in Greensboro [North Carolina] sat down at a segregated lunch counter and ordered coffee. Though they were refused service and were physically and verbally abused, they would not budge." Thus began the sit-in movement, which spread from the South to the North, rolling back segregation in many public accommodations. Inspired by the sit-ins, some participants organized the Student Nonviolent Coordinating Committee (SNCC) in the fall of 1960. In the face of angry white mobs, SNCC members challenged the status quo, all the while singing the anthem of the Civil Rights Movement, 'We Shall Overcome.'" Norton, Katzman, Escot, Chudacoff, Paterson, Tuttle, *People and a Nation: History of the United States.* (Boston: Houghton Mifflin Company, 1986) Vol. 2. 862. The SNCC disbanded in 1970.

4. Building on the SNCC Freedom Summer voter registration drive of 1964, the SCOPE project had three parts: voter registration, community organization and political education. Registering voters was one thing, but registering voters who understood the electoral process was another. Under the direction of Hosea Williams, this project intended to register voters, explain the electoral process and help the new voters understand how winning the ballot could help improve the communities in which they lived. For ten weeks, nearly four hundred volunteers worked under the direction of the local leadership with the assistance of local community workers and SCLC field staff. We were student volunteers, usually from northern colleges and universities from across the United States. In order to prepare inexperienced students to meet SCOPE's goals, SCLC provided a six-day orientation, which brought together speakers from the Civil Rights Movement, labor unions, the federal government, university professors, writers and the American Civil Liberties Union. Student volunteers were divided into teams of four to seven (usually from the same university), which were sent to rural and urban counties in the South. The project was timed to prepare voters for the passage of the Voting Rights Act of 1965.

my decision to go south in the summer of '65." Besides, Nellie's husband was studying for his Ph.D. exams that summer and she had no job. She saw a flyer at Stanford University calling for recruits and decided that the SCOPE project was the way she could follow in her sister's footsteps.

Julie TenBrink had a different story. She, too, is white and when I contacted her seeking her memories, she said she was a daddy's girl. Her father was dedicated to making changes in society and belonged to several peace organizations. Through one of these connections she learned that a male volunteer had backed out of the SCOPE project because it would be too dangerous, and she chose to take his place. She says she viewed it as an adventure as well as the right thing to do, and by doing it, she could support her father whom she loved very much.

Ray Nelson, a young white man from Arkansas, was a student at the University of California, Berkeley, in 1965. When I contacted him recently, he wrote, "I have always believed that our being in South Carolina was what we had to do. The issue for me was as much my own dignity and integrity as it was justice for black people. I have drawn strength from that. Even so, I think I had forgotten how intense the experience was for me and how complex the connection I had with classmates, community and family."

The trembling would eventually become action as my dignity and integrity found a focus: justice for black people. The spark: my U.S. History teaching assistant at Berkeley. When the news covered plans for the Selma-to-Montgomery March, he apologized that he would not be conducting class the next week. He was going to march in Selma. If he could do it, why not me? I never saw him again, but I walked out of his class feeling settled and tremble-free. Within an hour I'd signed up to get information on the SCOPE project.

Did I expect that something I did would change the world? In truth, I wasn't sure, but it didn't make any difference. I tried because, if I didn't, I wouldn't be the daughter my parents had raised and I wouldn't be the person I wanted to be.

You Came Here to Die, Didn't You

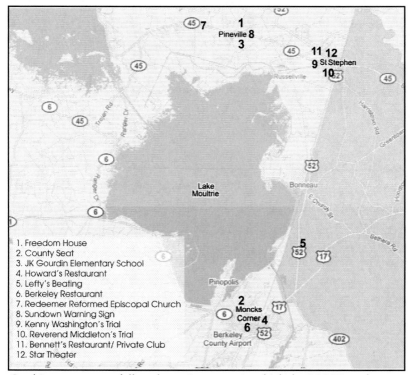

1. Freedom House
2. County Seat
3. JK Gourdin Elementary School
4. Howard's Restaurant
5. Lefty's Beating
6. Berkeley Restaurant
7. Redeemer Reformed Episcopal Church
8. Sundown Warning Sign
9. Kenny Washington's Trial
10. Reverend Middleton's Trial
11. Bennett's Restaurant/ Private Club
12. Star Theater

On this map you can follow the major events in which the SCOPE workers participated.

IN THE BEGINNING

ATLANTA, GEORGIA
Monday, June 14, 1965

"You came here to die, didn't you." It isn't a question. It's a challenge from a scrawny Negro[1] teenager in faded bib overalls. His bare chest glistens in the hot Georgia sunshine. He reeks of body odor and my stomach lurches as I look up at his black eyes, then down to his unshod feet in the grass.

I'm standing on the sidewalk at Morris Brown, a Negro college in Atlanta. The Civil Rights Movement is front-page news across the United States. As an eighteen-year-old, white, female voter-registration volunteer from California, I'd expected to be applauded upon arrival for a week of voter-registration training. Instead of a welcoming committee and pep rally, only this young man's almost angry dare welcomes me.

"I'm talkin' to you," he snaps. I force myself to meet his eyes. "If you didn't come here to die, it's time you git back into that car and head back to New York, Chicago or wherever you come from."

---

1. Americans of African descent have had several appellations in the history of this country. In 1965, the black Americans I met referred to themselves as Negroes. White southerners called them colored, nigrahs or niggers.

His scorn deflates the bravado that brought me here. I'm disconcerted, even disoriented. All the way from Berkeley, my three companions—Ray, Carol and Julie—and I had talked about dying only in an abstract way. Suddenly this teen makes my death possible and I want to escape him.

But he forces my attention to him. "So, why's you here?"

"I came to help Negroes get the right to vote."

"What's in it for you?"

"I don't think I can be free until everyone's free," I cite a slogan that inspired me to come here and wonder if I sound as cavalier to him as I do to myself.

"If some nigger killed yor father, would you still think so good of *Negroes*?" He mocks me.

"I hope it wouldn't make a difference."

"You got a lot to learn," he scoffs, then walks away.

That's why I came! I want to shout after him. I know I have a lot to learn. The Southern Christian Leadership Conference (SCLC) knows they have a lot to teach white volunteers. Some of us, like me, have never even shared a conversation with a Negro.

His harsh welcome was not what I'd expected two months earlier when my acceptance letter from SCLC arrived at my dorm at the University of California, Berkeley. I was excited when I showed the letter to my boyfriend, Vic, that evening.

"It's my pleasure to inform you that your application for SCLC's Southern Community Organization and Political Education (SCOPE) Project has been approved and temporarily accepted," the form letter announced. I was to report to Atlanta, on June 14, 1965, at 9:00 a.m. for orientation and training.

Vic set his napkin on the table and looked right in my eyes. "I think you're a white liberal with delusions about your own safety. What did your parents say?"

"I haven't told them yet. But I'm sure they'll agree. I know what I'm doing."

"You've done what?" My mother's face blanched when I told them and she took a deep breath to keep from crying out. Her eyebrows folded together over her huge sapphire eyes and her hands shook as she lit a cigarette.

"SCLC accepted me for a ten-week summer program. I leave for Atlanta on June eleventh. I thought you'd understand," I said softly. "You said that people have to act if they think the government is wrong."

"People. Not my daughter. Not you."

"But, Mom, it has to be somebody's daughter."

"You're going where they lynch people," my father exclaimed out of fear and frustration. "I can't protect you there. We won't help you."

"I'm not asking you to."

"Where are you going to get the money to go south and live once you get there?"

"Vic gave me a hundred dollars and I know people who support The Movement will donate money. I need fifty dollars to get there and about ten a week to stay. "

"Your boyfriend gave you money to go! What kind of a boyfriend do you have?" My father's eyes widened in disbelief.

"A boyfriend who's committed to making this country better."

"Then let *him* go."

"He won't. He can't. But he believes in The Movement, so he'll support me because I want to go. He isn't happy about it either."

RURAL OKLAHOMA
Saturday, June 12, 1965

Now, a month later, it's my turn to drive while Ray, Carol and Julie, other SCOPE volunteers from Berkeley, struggle to sleep. As Ray's VW bug buzzes along Route 66 in the dark toward Atlanta, I have plenty of time to recall the look of surprise in my parents' eyes when I shared *my* decision a month ago. I know my mother felt ambushed. She's always been consulted when I had something important to decide.

I feel the unyielding steering wheel beneath my fingers and become aware of tears dripping off my chin. I'm an adult agent for social change, not just a teenager on a dangerous lark. I have chosen a perilous path on which to grow up, and guilt for hurting my family stalks me.

6/5

    Just a note about the way I feel about going this summer. First, I got a very sweet and respectable letter from George Grainger today. He won't loan me ten dollars for the trip. Doesn't believe in northern meddlers. I'm very glad he didn't send the money. He's made it very clear what he thinks about the Movement. I would be very disappointed if he helped finance someone in it. I wonder if, perhaps, I compromised my principles somewhat by asking him for money.

    Mrs. Smith, a very nice lady in my Spanish class, waited for me after the final. She's very worried about me—doesn't believe in what I'm doing.

6/6 – 6/9

    How wonderful it is to be loved—I mean really loved the way

An excerpt from my journal, written just before I departed for Atlanta

Julie calls sleepily from the backseat, "How much longer until I drive, Sherie?"

"About fifteen minutes."

"Good, because four hours is too long to go without a stretch."

"Julie, are we selfish or heroes?"

"We'll know in ten weeks. Stop at the next gas station, I've got to pee."

MORRIS BROWN COLLEGE, ATLANTA
Monday, June 14

Now that I'm here—in the very heart of the Confederacy—I'm sure I belong here, that this is my calling, although my stomach continues to churn with the memory of what the Negro teenager said, "You came here to die." But when Ray, Carol, Julie and I enter the gym and hear the freedom song "Ain't Goinna Let Nobody Turn Me Round" I'm drawn in instantly. I feel at home.

> *Ain't gonna let nobody turn me round,*
> *Gonna keep on a-walkin',*
> *Keep on a-talkin',*
> *Marchin' up to Freedom Land.*

Over four hundred young people stand facing the stage and swaying together as they sing. More than half are white, the others Negro. It's freedom songs like this one that will sustain us when we're tired, hungry and frustrated. They'll bond us together when we're afraid. They'll carry us through the summer, providing unity, strength and a common cause. Most of them are based on old Negro spirituals. Some have the same lyrics as the old songs, but others have new words to reflect the goals and actions of the Civil Rights Movement.

"We're going to be busy," Carol observes as we register at one of the tables along the back wall and see our schedule for the first time. "It's eight a.m. to midnight for six solid days. It's a good thing we gave up wearing makeup on the drive here. We wouldn't have time to put it on anyway."

"Did you get a sandwich?" someone asks, breaking into my daydream some eight hours later. I realize I've been piecing together what I've seen and heard. I hurry to the back of the gym and grab a peanut-butter-and-jelly sandwich. The next speaker on the schedule is Dr. Martin Luther King, Jr., and I don't want to miss any of his explanation of "Why We Are Here."

His impassioned voice called us from colleges and universities outside the South and whether it was his, "One has not only a legal but a moral responsibility to disobey unjust laws," or "Injustice anywhere is a threat to justice everywhere," we were moved by it. We are white and the SCLC leadership hopes this will make a difference. Americans don't seem to care that Negro teenagers and children are beaten with nightsticks, attacked with police dogs and swept away with fire hoses while demonstrating for the right to vote. But if one of us is injured, our white parents have access to the system of newspapers and television. We are willing to take a chance because Dr. King said, "It may get me crucified. I may even die. But I want it said even if I die in the struggle that, 'He died to make men free.'"

He appealed to my sense of righteous indignation. How could Negroes be refused the right to vote? Sitting in my dorm room in Berkeley, I listened as the voice of this nationally acclaimed hero urged *me* to decide to act on what was right. I don't know what it is to be Negro or poor or discriminated against. Caught up in the idea of a national movement, a community of soldiers united for a common cause, I knew intellectually the power of the ideas of free and equal and the romance of the historical moment.

But we are not to hear Dr. King's voice tonight. For some reason he can't be with us. Understanding our disappointment, a speaker explains that SCOPE is much more than a political organization. Many of us will enter communities untouched by friendly whites before. The impact of our living in and working with the community may be the most important thing we can do because we'll "walk the walk" making it clear that Negroes and whites can live together. That had never occurred to me before.

"Walking the walk" will be made more difficult because those of us who are non-southerners are used to a different rhythm and pace of life. The slower southern pace is obvious. Normally concerned about punctuality, I'm bummed out here because things don't start on schedule.

The Rev. James Bevel, Director of Direct Action, SCLC, conducts one of many Workshops on Non-violence for volunteers at the SCOPE orientation

Students at the Atlanta orientation listen to Reverend James Bevel.

Time is casual. It's more important to speak with a friend than it is to get the meeting going immediately. Frustration, not disappointment, is my response when Dr. King doesn't appear tonight. As students from major universities and colleges in the United States, we live by organization, deadlines, appointments and a system that moves on regardless of our ability to cope. There is a way to sign up for a class, a way to drop a class, a way to pass a class and a way to respond if you flunk.

A consistent structure for our lives is a luxury we won't have now. Here all plans, appointments and schedules are fluid. Everything depends upon the timing and the ability of those involved to make it work. If a car has a flat tire or breaks down, someone is beaten or arrested, enough money is not forthcoming or a county office is suddenly closed, our plans will have to be retooled on the fly. We're like pioneers on a wagon train. All we can count on is our ingenuity and adaptability. The lack of control is frightening. Could it be that I really am here to die?

"How will we remember all this information?" I ask the coffee-colored girl on my right the next morning. I notice she has no pencil or paper while I review notes in my journal on implementation of the Civil Rights Act of 1964 as though preparing for a final exam.

"We just have to trust the Lord will tell us what we can' remember," she answers with a grin. I wonder if she can read and write. Yesterday we filled out forms including one excusing the SCLC if we're hurt or killed. Many of the southern Negro volunteers just signed their names leaving the forms blank. When I mention this to Ray he says many of them are illiterate, and only know how to write their names.

"Then how will they get people to register to vote?" I ask. I'm shocked that in America there are people my age who can't read.

"Have you heard them talk? They know this stuff. Conversation is the key that will make them free. Reading and writing isn't the only way to know things. It's just an academic person's way."

Maybe the Negro students can't read and write, but they are passionate about freeing their people. Some withhold information to protect their families. Others have been disowned by their families for their involvement in SCLC, with fears of retaliation splitting families apart. These students, hobbled by the cruelty of racism, must function weighed down by fear, deprivation and the skin color they cannot escape.

The speakers say we're brave. I don't agree that we all are. My bravery is untested, based upon television news. They are the brave ones because they face fear they know and live. What's in it for me? Am I here for an adventure or because it is the right thing to do?

My only experience with segregation so far involves the gas station restroom doors once we entered the South. Although the colors might vary at other gas stations, the first one we saw had two yellow doors, one labeled Men and the other Women, just like at home. But, there was a third, a red door labeled Colored. The message was clear that colored people were inferior to whites and didn't deserve the dignity of separate washrooms for men and women.

We're learning how to file lawsuits if we encounter segregated businesses covered in the Civil Rights Act of 1964.[2] A second way to influence these businesses may be direct action: a picket line, a sit-in, a demonstration. Our focus is on voter registration, but we don't know what we'll find in the local community.

After dinner the volunteers meet in the gym and sing:

Everybody wants Free-ee-ee-dom,
Everybody wants Free-ee-ee-dom,
Everybody wants Free-ee-ee-dom,
Freedom, Freedom

Unexpectedly Dr. Martin Luther King, Jr., enters from the side door

---

2. On July 2, 1964, President Johnson signed into law the most comprehensive civil rights legislation enacted up to that time. It met the demands of the civil rights activists in several key ways.

"For example, the civil rights movement had protested the forced exclusion or separation of African Americans and whites in public places. Title II of the 1964 Civil Rights Act forbade and a standing ovation rocks the gym. Dressed in a dark suit, he looks like the pictures I've seen. But he looks so tired, as though the weight of responsibility hurts his heart and soul.

He begins with, "It seems strange to hear people say Negroes are stupid or illogical when we've listened to those who have spoken from this lectern the last few days."

And then his lesson begins. I feel he speaks just to me, that I am alone and his words are my lifeline. "As the Bible says in Matthew 5:43-45, you should love your neighbor and hate your enemies. But Matthew then tells us to love our enemies, to bless those who abuse us, to do good to those who hate us, to pray for those who treat you spitefully, and persecute you."

He explains our journey together in terms of Christian understanding. As in "Letter from a Birmingham City Jail" (published in 1963) he explains why the direct action of voter registration is necessary and our responsibility. He tells us nonviolence isn't cowardly, but being spiritually active against evil. Our purpose is to gain the people's understanding, not to hurt them. We must choose to accept others' actions without verbal or physical retaliation. "Act in the conviction that the universe is based on justice and that goodness will prevail."

No one in the audience stirs. He speaks with passion, but something is different, here, in person. I don't feel the same awe and inspiration I see in the ecstatic faces around me. Slowly I realize he's not recruiting volunteers this time. He's presenting a pep talk, a celebration of the importance of what we're doing in Atlanta. This time he's not on television and I'm beginning to understand how the situation has changed. I'm growing into the role I will play: a civil rights worker. Dr. Martin Luther King, Jr., is real and the barefoot girl next to me may not be able to read and write. This time my body is involved and the boy in the bib overalls has made my mortality all too real.

Some people, like the girl next to me, weep. Others pray. Resolve radiates from the faces of the rest. Dr. King steps off the stage to join a reception line including Ralph Abernathy, Hosea Williams, Bayard

---

segregation in hotels, motels, restaurants, lunch counters, theaters, and sporting arenas that did business in interstate commerce . . . The Act also relieved individuals of the responsibility for bringing discrimination complaints to court. The Act made bringing discrimination cases the job of the federal government." Nash, Gary B., *American Odyssey: The United States in the Twentieth Century*. (New York: The McGraw-Hill Companies, Inc., 1997) 687.

Rustin and several other leaders of The Movement. We wait in line, awed that we are about to shake the hand of a great man among great men. I will never forget their faces or the tender hand of Dr. Martin Luther King, Jr. holding mine.

I'm not the only one going through a change in attitude, heart and focus. I meet a young Negro man studying at Morris Brown this summer. He feels he must make a moral decision. Should he drop out of school to join The Movement, sacrificing the money his parents struggled to pay? Or should he stay on and let The Movement go by? I understand his dilemma.

My opportunity for an education at the University of California was more than my parents had hoped for. My grades got me into Berkeley and my mother got a job at the post office to pay to send me there. My folks were lower middle class and struggling and all they could afford was a tin house, sort of like a square Quonset hut, resting on two acres of rock, manzanita and poison oak in Shingle Springs, California, about thirty-five miles from Sacramento in the foothills of the Sierra Nevada. I was shocked and disappointed when they bought the place. At ten I thought it grim. The Air Force had built the house as a vacation cottage for some general. I had to stand on tiptoe to look out the windows. In time my dad would put rock on the outer walls up to the windows and then add siding to the eaves. He and my brother made the shakes for the roof. I was in the eighth grade when he was rocking up my end of the house. What I don't think he realized was that he had left a sort of little stone stairway to my window. I took advantage and would sneak out to see my boyfriend.

Regardless of what this young man decides, commitment and acceptance are called for here, so I don't voice an opinion, even though he wasn't seeking one. We're not functioning as individuals but as representatives of SCLC. Later in the evening, however, my journal reveals my battle with myself. I now know "techniques" for nonviolence. I'm surprised how much I actually want to test those techniques, like staying down if knocked down and curling up in a ball on the ground while protecting my neck with my hands. Or going limp if someone tries to move me once I'm down. Am I crazy?

Alone. It feels so good to be alone the next morning after two days of intense orientation. I'm under a magnolia during a rare, solitary hour with my journal on my knee reviewing yesterday's session on nonviolence. I contemplate the concept of physical violence, a conscious choice to hurt someone. It is against my experience and against my Christian teaching. If attacked, will I be able to follow the directions we have been taught? Will I fight back? Will I cry and run? Will I love the person who is inflicting pain and fear?

I understand in my mind what Rev. James Lawson, Director of Nonviolent Education, said yesterday in one session, but in my heart I can't.

"Violence," he said, "is force or power which seeks to give out suffering to the opponents, forcing them to change their mindset. It is a man-created thing." My translation is that if we are threatened, it will be because the white people in the communities in which we work want us to go home. If they make us miserable enough, they think we will leave. Our test is to have our minds so set we can't be dissuaded.

A short white girl with braids stands and asks, "How much violence can we be expected to withstand?" There is a general nodding of heads and murmurs of agreement with her question. Our hearts were inspired to come here to the training. Now we have to convince our heads with passionate arguments from people who live the lives of the committed.

"Nonviolence is relevant because it's contagious," Lawson continues. "SCLC is a Christian organization. We believe that Christ would turn the other cheek and that we should love those who misuse us."

Rising to his feet, an unusually well-dressed Negro of about forty asks, "And what if they are willing to kill all of us? Isn't it foolish to just give in to their violence?"

"Amens" echo through the hall and the air is heavy with dread.

"You might not be Christians," Rev. Lawson thunders. "You might not be religious. So, know this. The less violent you are, the less you can be accused of starting or continuing a fight. You maintain your position of victim."

The well-dressed man stands again, "How is it useful to The Movement for me to be beaten or killed?" A little applause ripples through the hall.

Lawson says that another reason for nonviolence is that violence creates a domino effect. If we fight back, others might be drawn into the confrontation supporting us or the person attacking us.

"However, we don't want you to be foolish," he cautions as he concludes his address. "Timing is important. If you are in front of witnesses or a camera, and someone assaults you, be nonviolent. We can use the media to show how civil rights workers are treated. But, if you are out in the country and a truck full of white men pulls up, run like hell. No one will be there to appreciate the sacrifice you make if you don't. If the men catch you, fight back if you feel you have to. You'll be in a survival situation and will have to decide the ethics for yourself."

"Please give us some specific strategies we can apply to avoid the violence you talk about," the same Negro man says. Many of the members of the audience ready their notebooks and pencils.

"What do you think?" Lawson asks. "How would you avoid a confrontation in your hometown?"

A red-headed Negro girl stands quickly and says, "We should be polite and not argue with people."

"That's right and it's hard to do when you passionately disagree or when you've been pushed by someone. Some of you have been in fights. How could they have been avoided?"

A well-muscled, young, white man comments, "When I was studying karate they told us to pay attention to the situation around us. If we know things are getting out of control, we can leave."

"Excellent." When there are no more suggestions, Lawson prompts, "That's a good beginning for the inexperienced. Some of you have worked in St. Augustine, Florida, Mississippi and Alabama. What are the basic rules?"

"Don't go out alone. At least go in pairs." This is from a tall white woman standing against the wall in a staff tee shirt.

From the far back of the room a Negro at the staff table calls out, "Freedom Houses are the planning center for local projects. Some of you may actually live at yours and some just report there for work."

A white woman next to him adds, "While you're working away from the Freedom House, phone in every hour or so. That way, if you disappear, they can start looking for you sooner." That truly jolts me and I wonder if sooner will be good enough.

A gray-headed Negro man in his forties or so stands up in the front row. "If you're knocked down, stay down," he offers. "If you get up, you may be considered the aggressor and be treated accordingly."

"Learn to protect yourself when you're down," comes from a burly black man in bib overalls. "Put your knees against your chest, bend your head toward your knees and hold the back of your neck. It isn't fool-proof, but it protects your internal organs, your face and your neck." He hesitates, "If you're lucky." The noise in the room stops and we sit in contemplation.

I'm so glad my parents aren't here. My fear that began on the first day is growing. Later, I find myself needing to pee when we role-play what to do. That is a sure sign that I'm afraid. Someone said the bars on the windows in the dorms are for bomb protection. Is that for real? I hear yet again the sweaty young Negro's challenge about death.

A LESSON IN ETIQUETTE

O ver a cafeteria breakfast the following morning several of us discuss the communities the SCLC's leadership might send us to.

Shelly, a white male volunteer from the University of Montana comments, "There are rumors we're going to Mobile, Alabama."

Alice, a white student from the University of Pennsylvania, comments, "I expect to be sent to some city. SCLC is usually involved in cities like St. Augustine, Montgomery and Birmingham."

"I'd rather go to the country," I offer. "Didn't you see the Freedom Summer[1] news coverage last year? That's my picture of real voter-registration work."

"Are you nuts?" Shelly says. "Sounds like you're planning a vacation and want to be guaranteed a real civil rights experience."

"We're all probably a little off," I say. "I can't believe part of me thinks this way or accepts the violence we might meet."

"That's why there are staff members who make the decisions," Alice adds. "Lord, help us be happy wherever they send us."

"And safe," says Shelly.

---

1. Registration workers from SNCC (the Student Nonviolent Coordinating Committee) and CORE (the Congress of Racial Equality) were treated brutally as they attempted to register voters in rural Mississippi.

"Amen."

Sanford, a Negro from Georgia, sets his tray on the table to join us and our discussion changes to the workshops we've been attending.

"Sanford, you're from Georgia. Where you live, is it true that it's rude to mention that a lady is pregnant?" I ask. That's what a speaker had said at the workshop last evening.

Sanford smiles at me, "Remember, Sherie, we's religious folks. Some things aren't right to discuss in public or with strangers. That's why they tole us not to swear or use the Lord's name in vain."

Alice says, "We're supposed to dress like the people in the community dress. But, if we're going to be canvassing, it's much more comfortable in pants and sandals rather than dress shoes, nylons and heels."

"But successful canvassin' means havin' the community on our side. Sherie here is from California," Sanford explains. "She could show up in a bikini and be comfortable, but that would be a 'deadly' sin here. And I'm not talkin' about the Klan."

"I could *not* show up in a bikini and be comfortable," I protest.

Shelly says, "You think you have problems. We have to shave and have haircuts. We don't want to be accused of being long-haired hippy freaks by Negroes or whites."

"Still afraid of the California contingent, aren't we?" I say, and we all laugh. "Seriously though, I'm so exhausted from learning so much I could hardly get out of bed this morning."

"So, why are you here?" Shelly asks.

"Carol, my roommate, ordered me to get up because one of our workshops today is about the South and the Law."

"They ain't no law in the South," Sanford says. "But we do need to know what to do when arrested and when we go to court."

"It would be easier to just let them kill us than to learn all of this," I grumble. "But I'll be thankful later, I'm sure."

"Let's talk about sex," we hear someone from another table say. We look at one another and smile.

"There won't be any!" Alice comments. "That one minister said, 'Don't get involved with the opposite sex at all.' He said such a relationship can be misunderstood in the Negro and white communities."

"Right," said Sanford. "Theys serious about never travelin' alone with a person of the opposite sex and color. It would be dangerous for both of you. Hey Alice, want to go downtown for a Coke after the last workshop?"

"Not on your life, Sanford," Alice says.

"This training is like a lesson in etiquette," I say, changing the subject, "I talk so fast I have to remember to speak slowly and . . ."

"And you talk funny, too," Sanford teases.

"That's because she's from California," the others chime in.

"It's embarrassing that the staff has to teach us how to get along with Negroes who don't like white people," Shelly says. "They don't like us, whites don't like us, and we aren't allowed to like each other until the end of the summer."

"And we volunteered!" says Alice with a laugh. "We better get to the gym for the morning speaker."

The next day is our sixth day here. In the oven-like, humid gym we receive our go-forth speech from Hosea Williams, the director of the SCOPE project. His main point is that the future of the Negro people and our country go with us now. Standing in circles within circles on the gym floor we cross our arms and hold hands with those on either side of us as we sing "We Shall Overcome," swaying together. I have never felt such love for my fellowman or so much resolve. We might not agree on many things, like the war in Vietnam, religion or politics. But we all feel passionate about what we are about to do. I realize that once I leave here my inspiration must come from within myself.

Without speakers telling us we are the salt of the earth, overcoming may seem less possible. I have learned so much. But I still wonder if any of it is what the black teenager in the bib overalls thought I needed to learn. I guess I'll find out soon. Julie, a volunteer from Modesto Junior College, Nellie from Stanford and five of the volunteers from Berkeley— Carol, Ray, Florence, John and I—have been assigned to Charleston, South Carolina.

WAITING ON THE LORD

CHARLESTON, SOUTH CAROLINA
Saturday, June 19

Fresh from orientation, four of us are singing "Go Tell It On The Mountain" as Ray stops his VW bug at a light on King Street, the hub of the Negro section in uptown Charleston. Although we willingly stuff the VW full of suitcases, it can't hold everyone going from Atlanta to Charleston. Some of our group ride with someone else. My butt hurts from five hours' sweating in the backseat on Nellie's lap and her thighs must be dead from my weight, but we're ready to save the world. All of us are white and Ray is outnumbered by four women. We survey our assigned community.

"Hey, Florence. What percent of these folks are already registered to vote?" Ray asks, revving the motor to keep it going. Tall, freckled, red-haired Florence directs our SCOPE team. It's incongruous to me that she is from New Zealand.

"Thirty-four percent. Only sixty-six to go." She laughs. "And, we've got ten weeks to do it in."

"My God, this is worse than skid row in L.A.," I say. Then I feel thoughtless and foolish. So many windows are broken or boarded up and the alleys are full of trash. Electric lines clutter the sky between dilapidated, tall buildings. I don't know why the lines are so astonishing to me. It's like they obstruct any vigor that comes with the sun's rays. Nothing could flourish in such a place. I was ten when we left the Los Angeles area and we'd always lived in the suburbs where the sky was free. Then we moved to the country where it was endless. Here, King Street is a tunnel that blocks out all healthy life.

"No votes mean few public services," observes Florence.

"But they could clean it up themselves."

"Sherie, have you looked at the people yet?" she reproves. "Do they look like they have the energy to clean up the town in this heat? Remember what they said in Atlanta about the effects of poverty and deprivation."

"I remember," I say, chastised, thinking to myself those were just words, this is real. At eighteen, I'm the youngest of our group. I can hardly believe that last year I wore a formal to the prom, took the SAT and spent days riding my horse. I wonder what these people do. How could God allow people to live this way when I have been so blessed?

"Who would eat in those cafes?" someone mutters.

"The windows are so dirty and there are flies everywhere," Carol comments. "Even if they fry the chicken, it wouldn't be clean." Her ivory skin is mottled by heat rash and her honey-brown hair is wrapped on top of her head to keep it from chafing.

We finally find the address and Nellie murmurs, "Thank you, Jesus," as we unwind from the car in front of a church. I have been sitting on her lap much too long, my arm braced against the open window. It surprises me that Nellie is married. How did she ever convince her husband she should leave California to come to South Carolina? A Negro youth leads us down the stairs into the cool basement. I shiver from the change in temperature. Esau Jenkins, South Carolina coordinator for the SCLC, reaches his hand out to welcome each of us.

"As you know, we've arranged for you folks to stay with three local Negro families," he says. "Tomorrow mornin' meet back here for yor canvassin' assignments." He hands Florence a piece of paper with the addresses where we will live. "Now, y'all remember what they said in Atlanta. It's up to you to bring the dream of votin' to the people of Charleston." We climb the stairs back into the heat of the day.

Nellie and I are pleased as Ray pulls up to the house where she and I will stay. Tenements fill the blocks between the sagging cottage where we left Florence and the Leonards' neatly whitewashed home. Flowers smile in the small yard.

Bags in hand, we pause on the porch to gather our nerve. These people have extended a welcome to us, but we know nothing else about them. Nellie knocks. About five years older than I, she has a calm demeanor I'll find reassuring in the times ahead.

"Good evenin'," a tall, sturdy, walnut-colored woman says as she opens the door. "Are you them civil rights workers?" She doesn't meet our eyes, but we're both aware we are being scrutinized. Uncomfortable, I feel like asking her why she invited us if she doesn't want us here. Then I notice a little girl about six hiding behind her skirt.

"Yes ma'am," we answer together.

"I'm Mrs. Leonard. Welcome to my home. Yor rooms this way." She turns and walks quickly down a hall. We follow, a little surprised to be escorted to our room so quickly.

She opens a door on the right and says, "You two will share this room." Windows allow the light in and a cheery patchwork quilt covers a full-sized bed against the wall. She explains that the bathroom is at the end of the hall and we'll have to share it with the family.

"That's fine, ma'am. This room is lovely," Nellie says.

"I'll sen' Janis after you for supper in a few hours. You can res' here 'til then."

"Thank you, ma'am, and thank you for allowing us to stay here," I say and she says you're welcome and closes the door.

As we hear her walk down the hall, I have to ask, "Is it ok that we're here? The house is very nice but, except for the curious little girl, I feel we're a problem for them."

"She probably has no idea how to talk to us," Nellie says as she sets her suitcase on the bed and sits down beside it. "It's a little like being in a zoo, and we're the animals everyone has come to see. They risk a lot just by having us here." She opens her suitcase and takes out her towel and soap, two of the items on our packing list from SCLC.

"You sat on my lap all the way from Atlanta, so I get to shower first."

As she leaves the room I open my suitcase, dig out my copy of *The Souls of Black Folk* by W.E.B. DuBois, lie down on the bed and read, "One ever feels his twoness, an American, a Negro; two souls, two thoughts, two unreconciled strivings; two warring ideals in one dark body, whose dogged strength alone keeps it from being torn asunder." And I'm concerned because I'm always nervous with new people, I think as I slip off to sleep in the hot, late afternoon.

My hands grasp the door frame in desperation as Mrs. Leonard tries to throw me out the front door. I want to scream but I'm afraid it will only bring someone to help her. I have nowhere else to go. Her little girl is in the background clapping her hands. Nellie touches my arm softly and says, "Sherie, you're dreaming. It's only Janis coming to get us for supper." I'm not even aware of where I am, but Nellie's soothing voice calms me. "It's time for supper. Let's go."

At the other end of the hall a door is propped open with an old clay jug. It was hot in the bedroom, but the kitchen feels like a boiler room. The reason: the kitchen stove burns wood. Like a huge toad, the cast-iron box squats on short curved legs along one wall. It's almost as high as my mother's range at home, but that's where the comparison ends. A chimney runs up through the ceiling. Next to the range stands a bin with wood and a cardboard box holds scraps of dry paper and wood chips. The range itself is an assortment of doors and spaces: firebox, oven and others I can't identify. A meal in this room would be a comfy treat in winter, but in the summer it's a trial. The room is empty, although the table has been set for two and the plates are full of grits, fried fatback, and collards with pork neckbones. I'd enjoyed grits at the orientation, and the collard dish is new and tasty, but the greasy fatback turns my stomach. In time I will learn to like fatback, the fat on a side of pork salted and dried then cut into strips, but today I almost gag it down.

As we seat ourselves Nellie comments, "We'll never learn about the family if we don't see them."

"Considering the heat," I answer, "I'd rather eat and run than sit around and carry on a conversation. This is the first night. We have all summer."

We are surprised that no one joins us. We eat in silence and consternation. We wash the dishes and return to our room.

When we arrived I was thankful that the house is clean and maintained. Now I'm aware I must share a bed with Nellie. I'm uncomfortable; I've always had my own bed and the idea of sleeping with someone else is disturbing. What if she touches me or I roll into her? At home I didn't stay with friends more than once if I couldn't sleep alone. We change into pajamas, get into bed and say good night. I turn my back to her and lie there like a board determined to hold myself in place all night. My resolve isn't as strong as my need for a good night's sleep and I eventually nod off.

⌐⌐

"Have you registered to vote?" Carol and I ask the neighbors on Charlotte Street the next morning. As we walk along, children stop what they're doing to stare at us with cautious, big eyes. I'm blond and Carol has light-brown hair. We wave at them or stop and ask them their names. The youngest ones hide behind an older brother or sister, but their eyes are still on us. Teenagers cross to the other side of the street and stare. Men sitting in the shade of trees undress us with their eyes before they turn away. We are uncomfortable with their attention and aware that, as soon as we walk by, they begin watching us again. As we step over garbage to approach a door, our noses are assaulted by the acrid smells of stale urine and decay. We knock, someone answers and we introduce ourselves. If they haven't registered, we must persuade them to do so.

This is the theory, but we are in the reality of 1965. These buildings are typical Southern architecture; long rectangular boxes several stories tall with verandas down one side. On the Battery, the glamorous section of Charleston, such buildings are tourist gems. Uptown, in the black section of Charleston, they are the almost worthless moraine of debris left behind by segregation and disregard.

It's hard to believe the oppressive heat has already arrived by nine a.m. and our nylons make it worse. Carol and I canvass Charlotte Street. Regardless of my dream, I'm glad we're staying with the Leonards. These tenements stand beaten and sagging. Perhaps they've never been painted or else they've peeled and weathered to sand and beige. The tin roofs are rusted and some have shifted off center and lean away. Broken stairways lead upstairs. Railings on second and third floors are missing or hanging off the buildings. There is uneven sand instead of a sidewalk. Garbage and debris fill the spaces between tenements.

"God has forsaken these people," Carol murmurs as she steps over oily rags lying on the sidewalk and avoids a pothole in the asphalt at the edge of the street. Carol wears makeup again: foundation, blush, eye shadow, eyeliner and mascara. I've given it up since it just runs down my face. She still looks crisp even in the heat. She deserves to, she spends time trying to look nice. I've already slid into survival mode.

The doors of tiny apartments stand open onto the verandas in an attempt to woo a breeze inside. Many doors open to windowless single rooms. Like prison cells, I think. Cracked woodwork and rickety staircases dare us to reach our charges. I check my list for a name, exchange a glance with Carol and we venture into one of these sweltering cells. A scrawny woman about fifty perches like a bird on a broken stuffed chair and fans herself with Jesus. Fans from church often have a picture of Jesus on one side and an advertisement for the local undertaker on the other. Her skin is blue-black and her wiry salt-and-pepper hair is tight against her scalp.

"Ma'am? Are you Mrs. Gadsden?" I ask. Her eyes are wide and fearful as she replies so softly I can't hear her. I move closer, then closer still. I ask her several more times and am embarrassed because I don't understand what she's saying, her patois much stronger than I have yet encountered. Carol asks her to spell her name. She spells "d c a b r g h" as she drifts off and turns her face from us. She can't spell her name. Chagrined that we have made her uncomfortable, we thank her and leave.

"They told us to expect this," Carol whispers as we walk out the door and onto the street.

"But they didn't warn us how we'd feel," I say disconsolately. "There was no training to deal with this horrible sense of desolation."

Finally, after twenty fruitless conversations in stifling rooms, Carol and I find a woman who is pert, cooperative and encouraging. Her name, she says, is Nell and she has coppery skin and unusually light gray eyes. There are a couple magazines on a tiny table and the room is neat and clean. We are confident that we've found someone who can actually register.

"Ah wants to vote if y'all says Ah should, but whats votin?" she asks.

"It's when you go to the polls and write down the name of the person you want to put into office," Carol slowly explains.

"What are polls? Ah ain't seen them. Where can Ah finds one?" Nell smiles engagingly, "Do Ah has to read and write to use them polls? Ah didn't get pas' second grade and Ah can' write." Carol and I exchange a disappointed glance.

If we could stay for months, we might actually help Nell reach the polls. But, we can't, so we thank her and she walks with us to the street.

"Be sure you comes back when you can learn me more," she calls as we cross the street.

"We will!" we call as we wave good-bye.

"And, we've been trained to expect folks like Nell," I say, slightly encouraged. "We have to be sure we give her name to Florence to pass on to whoever runs the Freedom School."[1]

"Absolutely," Carol says. "She can register if they can just get a chance to teach her how. I have such a headache from this sadness."

On the third block the stench of death staggers us. Carol's face turns ashen and she covers her mouth, "Oh my God, what is that? I can't go any closer."

"But we said we would cover this block." I don't want to go either.

"You can go, but I'll work another block." I watch her flee down the dusty street as I stand suspended between flight and a promise to myself. I submit to the unknown and approach the first building as though a monster dwelled within. I turn into a side yard, and am careful as I navigate the broken concrete walkway, cracked by tree roots. I walk up to the first open door and knock softly on the jamb. The stench emanates from here, but I force myself into furnace-hot air and fight the upheaval in my stomach. Only a broken louvered door propped open with a chunk of gray concrete allows light and air into her windowless stall. I consult my list and whisper, "Mrs. Dingle?"

"Yaas, ma'am." Was that sigh actually words? As my eyes adjust to the darkness, I see a Negro woman lift her head from the bed, which is spotted brown with dried blood and excrement. My body freezes but my eyes are riveted on her leg, swollen to an enormous balloon, blistered, ulcerated, infected, the raw red sore filled with flies, their wings beating against her dying flesh.

---

1. "Beginning in the 1960s a new and determined young army of college students of all races and religions entered the South to teach a new freedom to long-oppressed Negroes. These new 'carpetbaggers' were trained in nonviolence and came armed with thick books and high ideals.

"They helped the local Negroes establish libraries, community centers, and 'Freedom Schools.' Their classes met under trees until rooms could be found. Negro children learned to read and write, to understand the rights of American citizens, and the role that Negroes have played in American History." Katz, William L., *Eyewitness: The Negro in American History.* (New York: Pitman Publishing Corporation, 1967) 491.

"Ma'am, Ah's waitin' on the Lord to take me home," she whispers as I stumble backward out the door. I vomit and vomit, but I cannot expel what I have seen. If I had known, would I have come? Now I know, but what can I do? My desire to run away overcomes my shattered hope of helping her. Dying would be easier than learning about all this. I came to help, but I have no idea how to.

⌒⌒

At the end of that first day, stunned and silent, we all meet in the church basement like survivors of a terrible storm. Ray looks up as I walk in. His brown hair is plastered to his head, his once-cheerful eyes are red rimmed and his face is wet. "Are you all right?" I ask.

"I can't do this." He looks back down. "They need so much more than voting. The poor children are . . ." his voice trails off but his hand gestures a sense of total loss.

Carol and Nellie come in less than five minutes later, pale and haggard. Carol collapses heavily onto a folding chair and says wearily, "After I left you, I found an ancient man tied with an old rope to a chair on a veranda. A neighbor said he was crazy in the head, and there was nothing else to do when his son had to go to work. He was just tied there all day. You could see he'd messed himself. Oh, Sherie, it was so awful."

We hear Florence upstairs imploring Esau Jenkins, the South Carolina director of SCOPE. "Work must be done here before voter registration can go on. Sherie found a woman dying alone from a rotten leg. We need literacy classes for the adults and a Head Start program for the children."

"To get them things, we mus' have power," he points out. "And to get power, we mus' get people to vote. Without the vote, we are a forgotten people. That's what they try to tell y'all in Atlanta." He is life tired. We have just discovered what he has spent a lifetime knowing.

"But what can we do for the woman?" Florence insists.

"Give her name to the church secretary an' she'll look into it, but there are thousands of Negroes sufferin' from sicknesses in Charleston. If they don't have a church, if their children have moved north, if they have no money, they slip on by. These folks do the bes' they can, but white folks don't care and they stops the poor from gettin' services they should.

If you ax that lady if she gets help from the government, she mos' likely say white folks tole her all the money was already gone. We talk about the right to vote because it's the only way we can get the right to live."

"Where's Julie?" Florence asks as she enters the room.

Ray says softly, "She's upstairs lying down. She was so sick."

"This is so much more awful than I thought it could be," I say as much to myself as anyone else. "It's like even God has abandoned them. I don't think I have the guts to go out again tomorrow." I'm disgusted with myself. My clothes stink with the hopelessness and death of Charlotte Street.

We look bleakly at one another, our innocence betrayed. If we run, we deny ourselves. If we stay, there will be no escape from the needs of the people on Charlotte Street and all the other streets and roads of the American South. Mrs. Dingle is waiting on the Lord so she can be at rest. The Lord is waiting on us to rise to the occasion.

AHA, SO THAT'S HOW IT FEELS

I know the child is here. I've sensed her presence each morning when sunshine peeks between curtains fashioned from scraps of cloth lovingly and repeatedly stitched together. Today, our fourth and last day in Charleston, I listen to her breath as the light filtering through a jar on the dresser bestows a prism on one of the whitewashed walls. The day is already warm and I kick the sheet aside. The aroma of fatback sizzling on the stove reminds me of waiting responsibilities. Others in the household are awake and busy, while I lie in bed contemplating a litany of the day's activities. I feel she is very close.

Her hand strokes my hair hesitantly. I choose not to interrupt her exploration and I keep my eyes closed so as not to frighten her away. The touch strengthens as she combs my tresses with her fingers and gathers some into a small hand-sized ball. Collecting another fistful, she presses her palms together, her fingers tangling into a knot. Aha! So, blond feels like this.

"Janis, you get yor bad self in here," her mother's voice intrudes from the kitchen. With a sharp intake of breath, Janis carefully untangles the strands so as not to pull my hair. She doesn't want to wake me and she doesn't want her mother to know where she is. A floorboard creaks as she darts out of the room.

Janis, I know now she is six, needs to know what white feels like because she has never been "touching" close to a white person before, separate but equal. She's too young to realize she wants to break the rules, the societal laws that dictate how colored people should relate to white people. If she ignores those customs, she risks punishment. The belief that she is definitely not equal is the foundation upon which these tenets, spoken and unspoken, stand. She may not walk on the sidewalk if a white person strolls there, she must step into the street. She may not sit at a table with a white person, enter a white restaurant through the front door or sit any place other than the colored section. She may not try on clothing or shoes in a white store because the clothing would be tainted. She must drink from the colored fountain and sit in the colored balcony at the movies. Even courtrooms are segregated. She could not have learned all the restrictions by the age of six, so her mother has commanded her to stay out of our way and to have good manners. Janis intuits that touching a houseguest is not good manners, but six-year-olds are not as inhibited as adults when it comes to satisfying curiosity.

That is what she is here to do. Her sable skin glows. Jet eyes question and laugh. Black pigtails adorn her head. Tan colors the palms of her hands and the bottoms of her feet. She delights in our differences. My blue eyes and white skin, not even tanned from the summer sun yet, tempt her. My lifeless, Marilyn Monroe mane slumps to my shoulders. Outside the bed clothes, white colors my hands and feet. And then there's Nellie, doe-eyed, with black-rimmed glasses and shorter dark-brown hair pulled back just behind her ears. We are white and she knows she mustn't touch us, but she is curious.

She perceives more about us than her siblings or her parents because she's not yet dipped into fear and despair. Although her parents, the Leonards, volunteered to put up civil rights workers for the summer, the culture of race is a barrier walling out any quick lessons about us. When Nellie and I sit at the kitchen table to eat, we eat alone while Janis's mother and sisters wait on us. It's like we have a room down the hall in a luncheonette.

"Mornin', ma'am. How y'all feeling?" Mrs. Leonard says, as Nellie and I take our places at the table spread with fresh biscuits, grape jelly, fatback and grits. Chipped plates hold our food and jelly jars serve as glasses. The yellow tablecloth is worn but spotless.

"Mornin'. How are you today?" Nellie offers.

"All right. Thanks," she answers as she heads to the back of the house.

Once she exits, Janis appears and squats across the room, watching us, then she sidles over next to me. When I appear involved in eating, she stretches out her hand and caresses my shin to see what white feels like. Older kids and some adults were even brasher than Janis. Some would say, "Can I touch you? I ain't never touched a white person befo." Once a Negro beautician offered to style my hair for free, "Just sos I can feel it in my fingers."

"Janis! What you doin', girl?" her mother scolds as she enters with a jug of water and refills our glasses. "Git out back an' help yor sistah with the clothes. Leave these ladies alone or I'm goin' tan yor hide."

She apologizes to us, "I can' git that girl to do nothin' I tells her." And she, too, leaves.

After breakfast we start to clear the table as we have each morning. And again, as though we had rung a bell, Mrs. Leonard returns.

"Don't you bother with them dishes. Y'all go off and do yor voter registratin' work."

We retreat to our room down the hall, closing the door behind us.

Nellie turns to me and whispers, "It's not right. We came here to help Negroes vote and have a better life, not to have them wait on us."

"I know. I want to tell them to forget we're white; just treat us like Negroes."

"But, we're not. If we say that, they'll be even more uncomfortable with us." Nellie sounds sure. "I hope we have enough time for them to come to trust us."

"I hope that happens soon. I hate it this way," I say as I pick up my canvassing directions and her notebook. I wish we could find a way to connect on a personal level with Mrs. Leonard without forcing her to break the rules she's followed all her life. She must believe in the Civil Rights Movement or we wouldn't be here. She took the step of opening her home to whites. If only we could find a way to encourage her to be our equal, not our servant. Thanks to Janis's exploration, I have learned, too; aha, so Negro skin feels the same as mine. But, what does it feel like inside to be a Negro in 1965? That's what I'm burning to know.

THE ROADBLOCK

———

RURAL BERKELEY COUNTY, SOUTH CAROLINA
Thursday, June 24

Who would believe we'd go from Berkeley, California, to Berkeley County, South Carolina? I mull over the futile effort of the last six days in Charleston as John, Nellie, Florence and I drive northwest on State Highway 52 toward Pineville, South Carolina. I'm disappointed, disillusioned and ready to go home.

"Why are we leaving Charleston?" Nellie asked Florence when she and John picked us up. John also came from Berkeley, California.

"The NAACP called and asked for workers for Pineville," Florence replied flipping through the satchel of papers she always carries. "We were free, so we got picked."

The past two days, bored and useless, we waited in the church pews for assignment. SCLC sent us to Charleston, but the National Association for the Advancement of Colored People (NAACP) directed the action there and they wanted us demonstrating for integration. If demonstrators are jailed, the NAACP could test the application of law in court. When the NAACP won a case, the locals enforced the law, theoretically. However, SCLC figured that if jailed, we couldn't register voters. Pineville, in the backwoods, was their answer.

John took advantage of those two days to buy a nine-passenger Pontiac station wagon to carry canvassers out into the countryside. Florence parted with the $800 grudgingly because it was a hefty chunk of the money raised in California to fund our project. We'll find that John's mechanical skills with alternators, plugs, carburetors and flat tires are essential to keeping our project mobile.

"Who knows anything about Pineville?" I inquire from what seems like a spacious backseat. The Pontiac is definitely bigger than Ray's Volkswagon.

"It lies between Lake Moultrie and Lake Marion out in cotton country. Like Charleston, it's in the Low Country or the low-lying areas of South Carolina," John says. "Otherwise, absolutely nothing."

Florence offers nothing more. I'm left to wonder: out of the frying pan, into the fire?

Countryside worthy of Monet—green fields of corn and cotton, dirt roads, pine groves, and creeks—lulls my attention as I contemplate the search for voters in a rural area. Lost in thought, I miss the sign when we enter Berkeley County and John's exclamation shocks me awake.

"Uh-oh!"

"Roadblock," Nellie mutters ominously and our heartbeats escalate.

God, for us? I wonder.

When Florence told us we were going to Pineville, she said that Reverend Blake, the minister who gave us our new assignment, had warned that all hell would break out when we arrived in Berkeley County. But, it's too soon. The Ku Klux Klan couldn't know we're coming, could they? And now we're stopped at a roadblock.

"Mornin', folks. Step out of the car, son. Bring your registration and license with you," demands a stern-faced, gray-haired white man with a clipboard who struts up to John's open window. Florence reaches into the glove compartment for the registration as John pulls his wallet out of his pocket, turns off the ignition and opens the door.

"Good morning," John says and follows the man to the front of the car. The man writes down information from the registration, license and license plate. They come back and John gets back in.

"You just bought this car?"

"Yes, sir."

"We're doin' a highway survey. What brings y'all to Berkeley County?"

John Kimball and
the Pontiac

"We're on vacation visiting family in Columbia." Good thing John knows one way to Columbia is through Berkeley County.

The man's penetrating eyes scrutinize Nellie and me in the backseat. "Step out of the car." We obey. He climbs in and checks the middle and backseats. "Where's your identification?"

We climb back in and dig into our purses. He writes down the information he wants. Some survey, I think. Who does he think he is?

Florence steps out of the car with her ID in her hand and smiles, "How far is it to Columbia from here?"

Ignoring her he walks to the rear of the car to examine our suitcases.

Without permission he opens the back, removes the suitcases, opens and searches them casually, then replaces them.

"Where y'all from?" he asks gruffly when he returns to take down her information.

"We're students at the University of Florida." John sounds absolutely sure.

"Well, while y'all are here ya should see Francis Marion's grave. He was called the Swamp Fox during the Revolutionary War, you know. Take

Highway 45 west from St. Stephen 'til ya pass Pineville and there's the grave on the right. Ya can see Santee Swamp, too. Then y'all come to the main highway. It's more direct than this one and ya git to Columbia in about an hour from there."

"Thank you, sir. Is there anything else?" John asks as we climb back into the car.

"Be careful what y'all do, son." He squints into the car and steps back, staring at us.

Silence. Then I hear the others breathing. John turns on the ignition and shifts gears to drive slowly through the roadblock.

"What's the speed limit?" he demands.

"Fifty," Nellie quickly answers. Too fast or too slow could get us stopped by the sheriff. Jail is dangerous for civil rights workers and an experience we dread. Despite the sodden heat, my hands are cold and I shiver in the backseat when I think of Negroes and civil rights workers who have been murdered and committed to swamps.

"Did he believe us?" In my dry mouth the words stick to my tongue.

"Let's hope so. If it wasn't a survey, the Klan knows we're here now, names, license-plate number and all," says Florence.

"Who the hell does he think he is?" I ask. "He wasn't even a cop. How could he treat us like that? It's like Nazi Germany here."

"Would you believe he gave us directions to Pineville?" Nellie comments.

"And to the swamp," I add, but my mind is on being ordered out of the car, on giving information to an unofficial stranger, on the indignity of feeling I had no choice but to comply. I'm not scared of the swamp, but I am irate. This is the first time I've felt cowed. Then I realize Negroes experience this disrespect daily and much worse. That's why I'd come. There's no turning back.

Fifty miles from Charleston to Pineville, but 100 years back in time. Mules pull wagons loaded with cotton, corn and tobacco along the two-lane country road with a faded centerline. Pineville, I later learned from the South Carolina Department of Archives and History, was once a "densely settled village" with a large white population but at the end of the Civil War much of the town was destroyed by Union troops and the land converted to farmland.

Berkeley in 1965 is a "black belt" county where the majority of residents are Negroes. The Pineville community is entirely Negro and folks work the fields pulling cotton sacks, picking corn and cutting tobacco leaves in the oppressive sunshine and humidity. An occasional cement-block building serves as a small market and churches occasionally dot the open farm and hunting fields.

John pulls into a small parking lot before a cement-block store.

"We're here," Florence announces as John kills the engine. For a minute we take in our new location. A two-story, cement-block building stands to the left of the store and beyond is a house built of the same material. All three buildings are painted white with weathered green trim. This is more encouraging than Charleston's slums and sadness.

A door-mounted bell rings as the green screen door of the store opens and slams behind two skinny little girls. They skip across the parking lot, see us and stop dead to stare while we leave the car.

Eyes wide with curiosity, feet bare in the dust, they watch us enter the store. The gap between the screen door and doorjamb allows flies to buzz on the crumb-strewn counter. An imposing middle-aged woman, black

Florence Jones, buckboard, and mule

The girls slept upstairs in the loft behind Carol Sanders and John Kimball.

hair pulled back tightly from her coffee-colored face, appears at the sound of the bell. With a firm librarian-like attitude, she steps out from behind the counter and says, "Florence Jones?"

As Florence moves forward and extends her hand, the woman announces, "Mrs. Martha Prioleau Simmons. Ah'm so glad the Lord brought y'all here. Ah feared no one was comin' to help us."

"We're here to do what we can," John says. I take in the inventory and notice sodas, honey buns, rice, laundry soap and a meager selection of other items.

"Oh, there's a lot to do," she answers. "It will be a busy summer for all of us. Aah was able to get that old green Ford in the parkin' lot for ya'll to use for canvassin'. Let me show you where y'all stay."

We three girls smile at our new accommodations—a spacious loft on the second floor of the two-story building sandwiched between the store and Mr. and Mrs. Simmons's house. Three double beds line up along one wall overlooking the parking lot. We'll have to stand on a bed to see out the windows, but sunlight fills the room. John, on the other hand, is relegated to one of three dark cubicles forming an L behind the store.

We are to find out later that Mrs. Simmons brought us here through an act of sheer will. When SCLC announced their summer voter registration program, she contacted them. Berkeley County is the third largest county in South Carolina and Mrs. Simmons requested thirty volunteers to canvass it all. SCLC promised thirty trained, white workers. By late June, none had arrived. When Charleston received nine workers, she put on her Sunday-go-to-meetin' hat, dress and shoes and went to Charleston. She intended to get the right to vote for her people. She also expected to get a return on the money she had spent on mattresses, bedding and supplies. Tall, full-bosomed and determined, Mrs. Simmons didn't hear "no" often. The day after her talk with the SCLC staff in Charleston we were in a car headed for Pineville.

Our arrival marks the establishment of a Freedom House, which is actually the store and two-story building belonging to Mrs. Simmons and her husband, George. They live in the house with Reginald, her son by a previous marriage, and her mother, Celi Mariah Middleton. We live on the property and hope that local workers will come every day to get voter registration assignments. Other folks will come with questions about welfare, papers they need deciphered, and legal questions. But we don't know that today. We consume our first dinner of plain white rice; grieve the lost world of fatback, collards and grits; look forward to a good night's sleep and pray for success.

George and Martha Prioleau Simmons

A VISIT FROM THE KLAN

PINEVILLE
Wednesday, June 30

Six days later, brilliant white light explodes against the night's darkness. I know this is an atomic blast and I automatically drop to the floor of our new office with memories of grade-school duck-and-cover drills in my head. It's not a bomb but only headlights. My terror doesn't know the difference at first. The confrontation we've expected has arrived.

"Snap off the lights," John, our second-in-command orders. "Shit! Nellie! Abraham! (Abraham is a local worker.) All these assholes need is to see a white woman and Negro man playing cards together. Get out of sight."

Afraid to leave cover, I slide from behind the desk and crawl along the floor until my hand darts up to the light switch. John steps into the open doorway, a black figure against the glare.

Pickup headlights are inches from the window as the driver revs the engine, threatening to smash glass, office, John and me. Other pickups line the front of the property. Blinded by the headlights, I can't see their occupants clearly in the dark, but I can feel their evil white presence. My heart pounds. I want to run, but my body is frozen in place. John stares them down, a lone figure against what we suspect is the Ku Klux Klan.

We hardly breathe watching the trucks drive off, their occupants hooting at us.

I start to stand up but a white body shoots past the window outside and I cower until Florence rushes in the door.

"What the hell was that?"

"It's about time," John answers. "We figured the Klan would make a run at us. That was the shot across our bow. Things are getting a bit more interesting."

"I'll call Atlanta and let them know the threat of violence has begun," Florence reaches for the phone and dials the number we all know by heart.

"We need to be ready from now on," John says. "Someone should be watching with a pencil and paper for taking down license numbers twenty-four hours a day."

"You're in charge of that, John," says Florence. "We'll take turns and local folks will help. Sherie, get on the typewriter and write up what you saw. I wonder what's coming next."

Since the "atomic bomb" incident, one of us begins each morning at first light lying in the grass sheltered under a pine tree where we can see the front of the office. We take turns on shifts twenty-four hours a day. Mule teams, their harnesses jangling, carry their owners to cotton and tobacco fields every morning. I ponder as I watch the road. It's 1965 and these farmers have mules, not tractors. This is America?

"Hey, girl, whatcha' seen this mornin'?" I jump at Maxine's drawl. She's one of our two paid local teenage workers. "You so jumpy, you think the Klan is after you?" Her teeth are white against her black skin as she laughs at me.

"I've seen nothin' but mules and wagons. Two cars went by last night, but they didn't even slow down. What are you doing here? I thought it was Butch's turn to watch." Butch is a student at South Carolina State College in the winter. He's been thinking about joining our project.

"You ain't heard about Butch yet?"

"What about him?"

Maxine shakes her head. "You know how his daddy doesn't want him doin' voter registration with us. Well, las' night the old man really discipline him."

"Oh no! Is he all right?"

"They carried him to the hospital. Tha's all Ah know."

"You said he'd be one of our best canvassers. His old man must be crazy." I want to cry. I'm so tired. It's been days since I have slept more than a wink. If I go to sleep, something more terrible could happen.

"Ah'm sure glad Ah don' live at this Freedom House. At least Ah can go home an' get away at night. You just has to stay and wait."

Maxine is right. I just wish I knew what we are waiting for.

Canvassing for voters

WHAT IF I FAIL?

PINEVILLE
Friday, July 2

Sweat trickles down our faces. It's nine days since we arrived and two nights since the headlight incident. As we scheme over wrinkled orientation notes and research folders strewn across the desk in our airless, cubbyhole office we realize we're stuck. Our problem: How do four white strangers inspire a Negro community to register to vote?

"Hey, are there any voter registration workers here?" a brash male voice bellows from the store. The new voice galvanizes us and we hurry out to meet a young, slender Negro in bib overalls and a white shirt.

"Hey, I'm Bob and this is Negro George," he says indicating his companion wearing Levi's and a blue cotton shirt. "We're a SCLC evaluation team from Atlanta here to see how y'all are doin' and to help if we can."

Florence, John, Nellie and I crowd around them to introduce ourselves. While Nellie goes for orange Nehi sodas, we lead them to the storeroom we use for meetings.

"So, honey," Bob says, grinning up at the taller Florence, "how's it goin' here?"

I cringe at his rudeness. Florence is our director, a graduate student from the University of California and at least ten years older than Bob. I thought this summer was about respect—respect for Negroes. Apparently Bob hasn't gotten the message that respect applies to women, too.

"I'll start at the top," she begins, her face reddening at his attitude. She explains that the local State Senator, Rembert C. Dennis, believes in the white school/black school way of life. Because the usual voter registration day fell on the Fourth of July, Dennis decided there wouldn't be a registration this month. But then, Mr. Holman, a local Negro undertaker, somehow convinced Senator Dennis to allow the registration books to be opened on another day."

"What do you mean 'another day'?" George asks.

"In order to vote in Berkeley County, South Carolina, an applicant has to go to Moncks Corner, the county seat, to sign the registration book. That makes him eligible to vote in the next election. The way the system works here there is only one weekday a month when this can be done unless a special registration day is called."

"It's a little over twenty-five miles away and it's hard to get folks there," John explains. "Fifty miles roundtrip in a buckboard is a long day. And registration days are always workdays."

"Each community has its own special problem." Bob asks, "Have you met the sheriff?"

"Now, Sheriff Hill is sly," Florence continues. "He sounded cooperative and assured us we would be safe this summer. But when we went to tell Hill about several drunken white men who came by hooting and hollering last week, he just said, 'Call me collect, **but don't let anyone see y'all here**.'"

Bob laughs derisively. "That sounds like a Southern sheriff avoidin' the situation," he says. "How about the schools?"

"Our visit to the Superintendent of Schools surprised us," she says. "They had Negro office workers. The superintendent offered all the information we asked for, even the budgets for the schools. But he shut us off immediately when we said we were registering Negroes. By then, it was too late though. We had what we needed."

"Do you have a youth group?" Negro George asks.

"Sherie is working with Mae and Maxine, two local girls, to pull a youth group together. Their first meeting is this Saturday night."

"Y'all got to get them kids revved up." Bob turns to me. "Their energy an' their commitment will give you four the credibility you need.

(l to r) Herbert Mitchell, Sally Kimball (John's visiting sister), Joe Swinton, Florence Jones, Kenny Washington, Joan Kennedy, and Henry Moultrie

An' find out if they want to integrate the high school. How about a Freedom School?"

"It's coming," Florence says. "We know how desperately these people need reading and writing. Once we start canvassing, we'll have a better idea of when to make appointments to help them be able to sign their names and find their candidate's name on the ballot."

"What have you learned about the local Negro leadership?" Negro George asks.

Florence tells him there are two NAACP chapters here. David Fashion is president of one and Rev. Fortune Haskell is president of the other. Pineville also has a community-improvement committee headed by Mrs. Simmons. Some ministers see our arrival as a threat to their power over their congregations, but Reverend Abraham Gadsden at Redeemer Church is behind our work and has allowed us to have mass meetings at the church.

"Here's the big question, honey," Bob says as he paces back and forth across the room. "What problems have you got?"

John says, "We've had our complimentary visit from the Klan. Several pickups parked out on the road, while one came right up to the window, headlights against the glass. They sat a few minutes to get our attention and then moved on."

"Hopefully that will be yor only visit," Negro George says. "But experience says there will be many more."

"Our biggest problem, though," Florence says, "is that we aren't Negro or inspirational speakers, as hard as we might try. We could use someone to make our meetings rock. A second issue is slashed tires. If we park in St. Stephen, the white-owned town about five miles away, or Moncks Corner, where the voter-registration office and county buildings are, we're sure to end up with at least one slashed tire. The Pontiac, in particular, needs constant care to keep running. We use it like we can trust it, but we can't."

Bob says he'll try to send out more help and then adds, "Baby, you have a bigger problem to deal with."

"And it is?" Florence says.

"Money. Yor budget was slashed by $400 an' Ah don't know why. Ah'm just deliverin' the message."

"Four hundred! But we were told to buy the car for canvassing. It took a huge chunk."

"There's more, have you considered bail money? If any of yor team goes to jail, honey, they'll need to be bailed out."

Florence pauses to stare at Bob. "If we're only working on voter registration, we won't be arrested, will we?"

"That's what we hope. SCLC figures that, out of all their projects in the South, as many as three volunteers will be kilt this summer. Local workers an' their families will be threatened with arrest for speedin', runnin' a stop sign, spittin' on the sidewalk, jaywalkin' an' any number of silly things. Yor white workers will face the same problems along with aidin' to the delinquency of minors, trespassin' since you're outside agitators an' incitin' a riot. If things get hot, y'all will need bail money."

"And funeral expenses? What if we don't have enough money?" Florence asks fearfully, trying to understand how deep the money problem goes.

"Families take care of funerals. Hopefully the work you've done with yor NAACP contacts will pay off any legal expenses," Bob finishes as he begins shaking our hands. "We've got to get on the road. Thanks for the sodas and conversation. Charleston's next on our list."

As Negro George hands me his empty bottle, he says to all of us, "It's bin a pleasure meetin' y'all. Y'all have taken the first steps. The project will happen." They cross the parking lot to their car, waving as they pull away.

"Well, that was depressing," Florence sighs. "Four hundred dollars gone with the wind."

"Negro George cheered me up," I comment. "We're doing what they expected."

"I knew organization would be loose and money tight." Florence shakes her head. "But I expected our main problem to be whites, not money. And I hate being called honey."

She frets about organization and money, and I worry about the source of enough inspiration to "rev up" the kids to challenge the world as they know it. The Lord gave us a registration day. The sheriff says he'll protect us. We've found a church in which to host the community. But, the problem remains, how do we get the people into the church? The youth group is where that answer lies, and it's largely my responsibility. But I have no clue how I, a white stranger, will inspire Negro teenagers to put their lives in my hands. What happens to our project if I fail?

Sherie Holbrook reading with the Snipe girls.

I HAVE A DREAM: ALIENATION

PINEVILLE
Saturday, July 3

"Please," I pray, "let this be kids," when the screen-door bell jingles at Mrs. Simmons's. But it's not and the door bangs hollowly as whoever came in leaves. Who am I kidding? I don't know how to direct a youth group. Maybe Florence picked me because I'm the youngest on our team. I'm young, and I don't know what I'm doing.

Our teachers in Atlanta urged us to use local high school students to recruit volunteers, so I'm excited when Maxine and Mae, our only paid workers, are interested in planning a gathering with me. Both are little more than a year younger than I and are in the twelfth grade. Mocha-skinned Maxine wears glasses and earlobe-length, straightened hair. In Berkeley, California, Afros are statements that change is coming. But here they are not yet in evidence. Our plan pleases Maxine, the more gregarious of the two. Mae is quieter and more serious, with a steady belief that life will turn out for the best. She's my height with russet skin; a pert, welcoming smile; and dark-rimmed glasses.

They will, they say, invite twelve of their close friends to a get-together. The three of us will explain how Negro children are getting a second-class education. The Movement and voter registration are the way to change that. This group would then plan a swimming party for a larger group. At that party we'll recruit canvassers for registration day this month and in the first week of August.

"They's a problem," Mae says, smiling regretfully.

"What's that?" I ask, deflated already.

"Most of my close friends leave in the summer."

"Why?"

Mae explains that students find summer work in Philadelphia, New York, New Jersey or Miami, since jobs are nonexistent in Pineville.

"Then theys folks like mine," Maxine says, "farmin' families who work hard all summer. Ah *should* be pickin' cotton. Ah couldn't be workin' here if y'all wasn't payin' me." Then she adds that some parents are afraid to let their children come because they fear someone involved in the project could be killed.

"What you're telling me," I sum up, "is we have to get teenagers willing to sneak out of the field and go against their parents' wishes."

"Yaas, ma'am," they chorus.

We'll see, I think and wonder how they could recruit their friends.

I agonize all afternoon about asking students to do something against their parents' wishes. How can that get the community to support the project? I fret about how to approach the kids until my head aches. I pace back and forth across the floor of our meeting room looking for answers. This back room used to be a juke joint. Maxine told me a *juke* is an African American word meaning a place for cheap food and drink—and for dancing. Whites, I reflect, might have called it a roadhouse and arrived by car, rather than wagon or on foot. If I could quit worrying, I could almost hear jazz blaring from a radio. But now the room smells of stale soap and mildew. On rainy afternoons we hang wet laundry on a line across the center and stacks of old books and boxes are stored behind the semi-circle of chairs. I wait as the hours drag by.

Suddenly the bell jangles, the door slams and Mae arrives. It's about five o'clock and her face glows with light makeup and a bow holds her bouffant hairdo in place.

"You look great!" I say, looking up from my list of topics to discuss.

"They ain't comin'," she says softly. "Theys a dance tonight an' everyone's goin' there."

I fight tears. I know I've failed this first assignment with the youth group. And I don't know how to fix it.

"Hey, Mae, Sherie," Maxine yells through the door. "Come on outside. Get Nellie and we can still go to the dance. Y'all can meet more people there than y'all could at this meetin'. Can y'all get the car from John?"

"Let's see," I answer on my way to the office to talk to him. John sits at the desk with his head in his hands, elbows on the table, reading a pamphlet on getting welfare benefits for folks denied them.

"I don't know, Sherie," John answers after I explain the situation. "You might do more harm than good going there. They'll be uneasy because you're white and this is a social gathering."

"Well, can Nellie and I use the car to take Mae and Maxine? We'll decide if we should stay once we get there."

Before he can decide, Florence calls an impromptu staff meeting and Nellie and I are stuck.

The next day Mae says, "When Ah come in las' night it was to tell y'all to come to the dance. Since the kids couldn't come to the meetin', they said y'all should come to them."

Maxine pouts as she adds, "All the kids were sorry y'all didn't come."

Now my stomach gets queasy thinking we've alienated the teenagers. Without them we are only four white canvassers.

Staff meeting

PENNIES FROM HEAVEN

PINEVILLE
Sunday, July 4, Independence Day

    The day after the youth meeting that didn't happen, Mae invites me to Hickory Hill Baptist Church. We enter and while I'm trading glances and tentative smiles with members of the congregation, although I don't know a soul, she disappears. Everyone is a Negro stranger and my heart sinks because this is my first church service without at least one other white volunteer. Here to meet people, I'm suddenly bashful and nervous. I can hear hushed comments and see eyes following me as I sit in the first seat I can find and scan the program for the day. The lady in front of me smells of lavender and holds a baby in her lap. The organist begins to play and I realize I'm on my own.

    Church is not the way my family celebrates the Fourth. I miss my father's barbecued pork ribs in the backyard at home. I haven't seen a potato in a month and the idea of one baked with sour cream and butter is distracting. Or how about a fresh green salad with blue-cheese dressing? My family has never been one for parades and fireworks but we do relish sharing a good meal. It's better not to focus on food, though, because it only reminds me of what I'm not having for dinner during the week. Our menu remains basic: plain grits for breakfast, honey buns and soda for lunch and lots of rice for dinner.

Once or twice the dark eyes of a slender, dark-skinned girl about my age meet mine from across the aisle. The organ plays the prelude and the congregation sings:

> *Amazing Grace, how sweet the sound,*
> *That saved a wretch like me . . .*
> *I once was lost but now am found,*
> *Was blind, but now, I see . . .*

The pastor's deep voice calls us to pray and as I bend my head, I feel the girl sliding shyly into the pew next to me. She is taller than I am and slender, dressed in a bleached white dress. I glance up and this time when our eyes meet, we smile and I'm warmed by her thoughtfulness.

"My name is Shirley," she says.

"I'm Sherie."

"Welcome to Hickory Hill," she says turning to participate in the service. The pastor talks about the importance of Independence Day, but he mostly expresses his fervent desire for independence for Negroes. Then he reminds everyone to register and VOTE! After the announcements, it's time for the reading of the Gospel and then the sermon. I need a Bible and hymn book.

But there's nothing in the book support on the back of the pew in front of us. Shirley has both books and she carefully shows me which to use as the rituals continue. More than that, she teaches me how to clap. Although I've been clapping since a small child, this is pattern clapping, different patterns for different rhythms, and I'm challenged. Most of the time I'm off rhythm and we giggle together until my hands catch the beat again.

I'm delighted just being with my new friend until it's time for the offering. This church doesn't pass a basket or plate. That would be easy. Instead the music picks up, the singing is joyous and the entire congregation forms a sort of conga line to carry their offerings to the front. Shirley indicates that I join her, takes my arm and tugs me into the line and I'm doing it, somehow my feet moving in step with those before me and Shirley behind.

Just before we reach the offering table I realize I have no money. I'm stricken. How could I come with no purse? I whisper my problem to her.

"That's okay," Shirley assures me.

When we reach the table she takes my hand and puts two of her five pennies in it—and smiles.

When I first sat in the pew I felt stranded and alone. Shirley offers me warmth, connection and generosity. In her care I experience the reason I'd come south: harmony and acceptance.

Shirley did not get involved in voter registration. Her mother wouldn't let her come to dinner with us. We were together for that one church service, and I never saw her again. But meeting Shirley was my Independence Day celebration.

(l to r) Gregory Sumpter, Nellie Habegger, Reginald Prioleau, and Jerome

WE DON'T GO BY THAT LAW
DOWN HERE: ARRESTED

PINEVILLE
Monday, July 5

"They've been arrested." Florence slams down the phone as Mae and I walk into our one-room office the morning of the fifth.

"Who has?" I ask.

"Four of the five SCOPE workers in Charleston."

"Which four? Why?"

"Ray, Julie, Carol and Joan. They were with nine NAACP workers who integrated Edisto Beach to celebrate the Fourth of July." I know Edisto Beach is on the coast about thirty miles from Charleston.

"My God, were they hurt?"

"No, but they spent last night in jail. Esau, our state director, is angry and wants me to come to Charleston to see what can be done."

"Why's he angry?"

"Because you can't register voters if you're in jail. Remember why we're here, no demonstrations, just registration. They go to court tomorrow."

I HAVE A DREAM: NEWCOMER

PINEVILLE
Tuesday, July 6

With Florence at the trial in Charleston, we try a teen meeting again the next day. This time we have invited all teenagers through the churches and word-of-mouth. To my relief, five girls and over thirty boys pack our room. I wonder fleetingly why there are so many more boys. Maybe the parents are more protective of their daughters. Guys usually do have more freedom than girls and they are more willing to skip out on what they're supposed to be doing. Maybe the girls are home sewing, cooking and taking care of younger siblings. But I have a bunch of kids and I'm ready to go.

Twenty minutes later I think it's worse than if they hadn't come at all as we sit in agonized silence. To each question I ask the group I get downcast eyes, blank dark faces and, perhaps, a nod or more likely a shrug. I haven't even created causal interest, let alone inspiration to act.

"Do your parents vote?"

"Can they read and write?"

"Have you been watching the news about the Civil Rights Movement?"

"Tell me about where you find jobs around here."

Waiting for a youth meeting *(l to r)*: Sherie Holbrook, Maxine Ravenell, Lula Mae Simmons, Joan Kennedy, and Nellie Habegger

It dawns on me that this monologue is frustrating and silly. They expected a party, not an interrogation.

Finally, a yellow-skinned boy raises his hand. I respond as if he's offering me a life jacket.

"Yes, what's your question? And please tell me your name so I can start learning it now," I invite lavishly, immediately aware that I've overdone it.

He watches me carefully for about twenty seconds as I struggle to sound normal.

"Ah'm Laurence. How can we go to white schools?" he asks.

"That's a great question. How many of you want to do that?" I ask. Maybe a dozen hands rise.

"Why go to school with crackers?" someone asks from the back. Everyone watches how I will accept this slur.

"Because they get better schools," Laurence responds. "Ah want to do somethin' with my life."

"Ah'm Bobby," the voice in the back continues. "Our schools are better than they were. My grandfather told me they were only allowed six months a year for six years of school when he was a kid. He missed two months a year of that 'cause he worked the fields, too." Bobby is a young man with a moustache.

"But, that was yor grandfather," Laurence objects. "Ah was tole that when they pass the law sayin' that schools had to mix Negro and white, the state of South Carolina choosed not to force Negro students to go to school at all."

"Then why we goin'?" Maxine asks with a smile.

"Because we have more sense than the state of South Carolina," Laurence says with some heat. I watch him and hope he will be the student leader we need. "Besides, our parents pay taxes to the state an' the county. Theys a bus for white kids, but not for us. We get to school any way we can. That's not right. Ah have plans but Ah can' do them without an education. White schools have better books, teachers an' buildin's than we have. Remember when we got 'new' books that had clearly bin used an' wrote in?"

"The thing Ah hate is lunchtime at school," Mae says sadly. "When Ah'm lucky enough to take a lunch, Ah hate sitting there with hungry eyes watchin' me. Some kids eat a baked sweet potato a day when they get home and that's all. Is it true that Negro an' white schools are so different?" They all turn toward me.

"We did some research when we came here. In the early fifties about $299 was spent per pupil per year for white students and about $169 for Negro students." I don't tell them that both numbers are grossly below that spent in California.

They sit quietly for a moment, doing the math in their heads.

"Let's go back to the original question," I begin. "According to the new Civil Rights Act of 1964 not everyone in every school has to be mixed until 1967."

"I'm Linda Darby. Ah thought kids were doin' it now," a serious girl says.

"They are. Anyone can attempt to go to a white school. But integrating the two school systems, one Negro and one white, is complicated, so the law gives school districts time to make all the adjustments. This year only freshmen and seniors have to integrate."

"No one told us an' several of us are seniors. We'll just go back to Russellville like usual," Maxine said.

"That's one of the reasons I'm here. You don't think the white board of education is going to tell you to go to white schools, do you? Just because there's a law doesn't mean it will be enforced. Did you hear about the Negro kids who went to white Central High School in Little Rock, Arkansas? They forced the school district to enforce the Supreme Court decision in Brown vs. Board of Education. President Eisenhower had to call out the 101st Airborne to get those kids safely through the day."

A girl with a bandana around her head says, "Y'all are crazy. If Ah walked up to St. Stephen High School, someone would shoot me."

"And that's the danger," I concede. "If you're turned away from the school, the NAACP will file a lawsuit against the school district. Eventually you will get in."

"Not if Ah'm dead."

"And that's the truth," I continue. "Right now you can be threatened and even killed. That's why we're here."

"Ya'll keep sayin' that," she challenges. "How can y'all help us?"

"I can't help you, but you can. Right now, white folks do pretty much what they want to because most Negroes don't vote."

"Whites won't *let* us vote. Theys so many restrictions an' it's dangerous."

"The Civil Rights Act of 1965 is coming this summer," I say, grateful to finally be using some of the facts I wrote down so conscientiously at orientation. That was only three weeks ago, but it seems like years. "It says those restrictions are illegal. If a Negro is turned away from registering, a *Federal* registrar, not the local election staff, can be appointed to register voters. That's someone backed up by Washington, D.C. That's why we need your help to get voters registered."

"How we do that?"

"Come canvass with us. That means talking to every person old enough to vote. If they're registered, that's great. But if they aren't, and most won't be, you need to persuade them to go and do it. The more people who vote, the more power you'll have."

"How they goin' to get to Moncks Corner to register?"

"We're going to have busses to carry them down there."

Laurence says, "Ah'm a senior. There isn't any chance for me is there?"

"Those of you who want to go to St. Stephen High School in the fall need to give me your names. I'll contact the NAACP and let them know you want some coaching," I say as I pass around a piece of paper and a pencil.

(l to r) Sherie Holbrook, Doris Rose, Jerry Dingle, and Brenda Rose

They fall to talking in small groups and I figure it's time for that party. I don't speak like Dr. Martin Luther King, Jr. I haven't been thrown in jail or beaten. I'm obviously a newcomer, but I do know something they want to know.

We call it a party, but it is mostly sodas and snacks. I didn't know until now how little social contact kids had outside of school and church. Mae turns on the record player and Wilson Pickett's "In the Midnight Hour" fills the room. Since this is the only record we have, I hope she asked someone to bring more. Last year when I left high school we were surfing to the Beach Boys. There is no relationship between what we were doing flailing about as though we were on surf boards and what I now see on the floor before me, intricate dance routines. I attempt to blend into the group playing cards, watching from afar, but a young Negro man with a gold front tooth, grinning at my obvious discomfort, asks me to dance. All eyes watch us. What will this white girl do? I know I'm blushing and I try to make excuses, but I'm being included in the group, so I shyly accept.

By midnight I'm beat and they're ready to go home. On the way out the door, six kids offer to canvass for us and several comment on how good the evening was. "Can we have another meetin'?" they ask.

I feel redeemed. I just had to "let go and let God," as the ladies at church might say. I'm thankful that He came through tonight.

HOGSHEAD STEW

PINEVILLE
Wednesday, July 7

How could I feel so elated at the youth meeting last night and so crushed this morning? It's only been about nine hours. The six kids who promised to show up last night didn't come in today. I'll get used to it eventually but today everyone is busy doing something else and so I sulk, refusing to canvass alone.

Then I see Deke, a Negro civil rights worker on loan from the Charleston Freedom House, walk into the yard from down the road leading a mid-sized, dull brown hog on a piece of rope.

"Where did that come from?" I ask with interest.

"Theys an old gentleman down the street wants to contribute to the project. He ain't got no money and he's too old to canvass. This hog's from him."

"What do we want with a hog?" The obvious still escapes me.

He laughs at me, "Makes somethin' wunnerful! Kills it! Eats it!"

I shrink inside. Where I come from pork is neatly wrapped in plastic. He tethers the hog to the tree.

Is he going to slaughter it right here? I can tell I must be paler than I

Deke with dinner

can imagine, because he gives me a grin and a "poor white folks" shake of the head implying I just don't know much about life or surviving it.

I walk over to the hog and look down at the condemned. Whispering, "Hi baby," I reach down to pet its snout.

"Git back girl," Deke commands. "We's goin' to eat this here hog. Don' go gettin' too friendly!"

He leads it over to a school desk turned chopping block. A borrowed cleaver rests on the block. Deke has spent part of the morning sharpening it and he tests the edge with a blade of grass and signals me to turn away. Determined to show him I'm tough, I don't turn.

He shrugs, bends down and slices the hog's throat. That was it. The hog doesn't make a sound; blood just pumps steadily out onto the grass as the animal shudders and slumps. Shocked, I stare as with a single whack, the head falls to the ground. Deke hauls the carcass to the woods to bleed out. We have enough flies already without an invitation.

When he returns, he expertly butchers the head into a mound of red meat, brains, eyes and all. Flies dance on the block, the meat and on us.

Deke reaches down for the pan he'd put on the ground and pushes meat, bone and bristle into it. "Now wash up this here blood," he directs me. "We don' wan flies all over."

I feel like Cinderella (well before the ball) cleaning up the remains and picking through the grass searching for fragments that would entice flies. Finally, with limited water pressure I dribble the water over my feet and hands several times—until the blood is gone.

Deke stops me at the kitchen door but over his shoulder I see he's already canvassed the neighborhood for fresh vegetables: a handful of peas, a pile of okra, half an onion, and a small bunch of collards. He has called upon several of our neighbors to donate what little fixin's they could spare. Like the gift of the pig, people show their appreciation for our presence by sharing the little they have. Any apprehension I might have had about eating a hog head is outweighed by my growling stomach and my head aching with hunger.

Our usual dinner here is a bowl of rice, which does not tempt or satisfy our appetites. The eleven dollars a week we pay for room and board provides us with what the local people eat most of the time.

Only on Sundays do we feast when someone from a church invites us for an ample supper: green beans, collard greens, iced tea or lemonade, macaroni and cheese, fried chicken, okra (fried or stewed), field peas, ham and cake so heavy and delicious we dream on it for a week. These meals help us to feel part of the family that invites us. Slowly our feeling of belonging to the community grows.

Tonight we'll delight in a meal from our own kitchen. Tonight only the Freedom House staff is here, but leftovers will be shared with canvassers when they come in tomorrow. Stew, brown and thick, bubbles on the stove in the cook room at the back of the store. Mingled aromas of pork, onions, greens and other fresh vegetables permeate the kitchen and escape through the cracks in the walls. Beckoned by the kitchen fragrances we white folks are seated at the table early and Deke presents his masterpiece, which we spoon over our usual rice. As we eat we pick out a bone fragment, a discolored tooth, or a bit of bristle and toss it into the bowl in the center of the table.

Deke laughs because he has created something "wunnerful" from what we white folks consider nothing—a hog head. What we consider to be creative and resourceful, Deke and Negro folks consider soul food, a simple fare made with the ingredients at hand, with nothing wasted, holding body, family and spirit together.

We are satisfied by the quantity and the fine preparation, unusual ingredients, and attractive presentation of what we eat. In Deke's world, satisfaction comes from *having* something to eat. This stew is a symbol of the differences in perception between us outsiders and the people from Pineville. We are used to "having." They are used to "surviving." It's dangerous for them to canvass, to be seen with us, or to register to vote. But, by feeding us, they can support us safely. Of course, feeding us means less for their families.

But that wasn't one of my considerations when I volunteered. I would have laughed if anyone in California suggested I'd actually eat the head of a pig. But this is one way to measure that I'm fitting in.

WE DON'T GO BY THAT LAW DOWN HERE: THE TRIAL

PINEVILLE
Thursday, July 8

South Carolina beaches beckon tourists with sweeping white sand before the expanse of blue Atlantic, sun reflected from the lips of waves. We'd seen the faded billboards engulfed in kudzu vines along the sides of the roads.

Come here to vacation in paradise. If you are white.

Colored tourists need not apply, arrive, share, walk or soil the pristine sands. The State of South Carolina chose to close state parks and beaches in 1956 to avoid desegregation. At one time a Negro could be fined thousands of dollars or years in prison for walking on a white beach. Instead of "White Only," the signs now read "Closed. No Trespassing." As far as we knew, only Folly Beach was still open. And we were told the whites who used it would physically defend it against any colored bathers. Pineville is too far from the ocean to care. We had swamps to swim in, but the Charleston workers had no place to wash off the sweat of the city.

Florence returned from the trial today.

"You won't believe the farce I just watched," she comments, sitting down at the picnic table behind our office. "The trial wasn't even at the courthouse but at the magistrate's house way out in the country at the end of a long dirt road. Rather than a slave shack at the end, like when we're canvassing for voters, there was this big, old, white southern home like in the movies. It wasn't a mansion, but it had a veranda around it and a dirt yard." She pauses wearily. "Get everyone out here so I only have to tell it once."

Volunteers and local workers sit at the table or pull up rusty folding chairs.

"Did they get off?"

"What do you think? They were fined $50 apiece or thirty days in jail."

"They don't have that kind of money."

"The NAACP does; they paid the fines. Would you believe, when the SCOPE and NAACP workers pulled up in Magistrate's Seabrook's front yard, he yelled from the porch, 'Y'all are a bunch of communists . . . outside agitators!' This was the judge! So much for a fair trial."

A new canvasser, Ishmael Prioleau asks, "Is he a judge or a magistrate?" Ishmael is quiet and has beautiful eyes.

"I don't know. He was called both in the trial papers and in person."

"Did he just say they were guilty and fine them?" I ask.

"No, there was a trial," Florence continues. "This was my first chance to watch Matthew Perry work. He's the Negro lawyer from Columbia who has been defending many of the civil rights cases in South Carolina. The NAACP hired him and two Negro lawyers from Charleston—Bernard Fielding and Russell Brown—to defend our folks. Brown bailed them out. I guess he bails out so many civil rights workers he carries a bunch of bail bonds in his pocket all the time, just in case."

"What exactly did they do to get arrested?" Nellie asks.

Florence makes a face. "They were arrested for trespassing because they walked past no trespassing signs twenty-five feet onto Edisto Beach. Some laid out a blanket. Some of them sat down on it and took out lunch. A couple of the gals walked down to the water. They saw the signs, but whites were on the beach and in the water ignoring the sign. A mixed group of Negroes and whites, our guys were almost immediately arrested. No warning, just arrested."

"Were the whites on the beach arrested?" John asked.

"Of course not, they were trespassing, but they were all white. You know they weren't arrested."

We all knew voter-registration workers and other activists expected to be found guilty. A Negro sitting down at a white lunch counter is breaking the law. A Negro who refuses to sit in the colored section of a movie theater is breaking the law. A Negro who walks on a white beach is breaking the law. A white person accompanying a Negro person is a "nigger lover" who deserves the same treatment. Once a federal law passed establishing that Negroes could do these things, the southern power structure did not step genteelly aside to welcome the new participants in freedom. In order for the new federal law to be upheld, someone had to break the state law. Whoever that someone was, they expected to lose. Appeal to a higher court, eventually a federal court, was the way law was really implemented. Case by case, from bailing out the lawbreaker, to defending him or her in court, to filing appeals, to paying the fees was the domain of the NAACP.

"And the trial?" John again.

"Let's say Judge Seabrook watches enough television to frequently call Matthew Perry, Perry Mason. But he hasn't watched enough to know how to conduct a trial, respond to motions or appreciate witnesses. Let me read you some excerpts from the transcript."

Florence thumbs through the transcript.[1] "Here, listen to this from early in the trial:

> Perry: Judge, I respectfully ask that you disqualify yourself as a judge to preside over these proceedings . . . Your Honor, I believe, referred to the defendants as communists . . .
>
> Judge Seabrook: I don't think it's necessary. I base it on the facts.
>
> Officer Harmon, the arresting officer: Judge, you need to respond to the motion from Mr. Perry.
>
> Judge Seabrook: Overruled . . .

---

1. Manuscript of the trial of the State of South Carolina vs. Barrett, Bryant, Kennedy, Nelson, Lawlor, Frasier, Saunders [sic], Gallashaw, Bennett, Miroff, Tenbrink, Williams and Daniels.

Julie TenBrink gave me a copy of the transcript. The night of the trial she helped type up that copy. I have been unable to find another. The Court Administration in Charleston, South Carolina, says that the transcript no longer appears in their records. It was destroyed years ago. TenBrink retains her copy.

Perry: [this is in violation of] the due process clause of the Fourteenth Amendment to the Constitution of the United States . . .

Judge Seabrook: I am not much on these small points. I jump over them.

Perry: The warrants don't allege a crime under the Laws of South Carolina.

Judge Seabrook: I have piles of warrants, and I have been a magistrate for twenty years and have never had a lawyer find fault with them. They all said they were all right.

Perry: Your Honor, do you deny my motion?

Judge Seabrook: Well, what are you after anyhow? I thought you wanted them tried?

Perry: No, sir, I want them dismissed.

Prosecutor Craven: Your Honor, counsel wants you to either overrule or rule in his favor. If you want the proceedings to go on, it would be overruled.

Judge Seabrook: I want it to go on.

Perry: You therefore deny my motion, Your Honor.

Judge Seabrook: I do, yes. I think I do, yes. Yes, you are talking Greek to me sometimes.

Perry: All right, sir, now may it please the Court, the defendants respectfully move the Court for a public trial. Your Honor, this motion, of course, is made with the full realization that your facilities here are not made to accommodate large numbers of people . . .

Florence tells us that the judge was initially perfectly happy to have the trial under a Chinaberry tree in the yard where it was cooler, but Mr. Perry wanted it moved into the house.

Judge Seabrook: You have one [a public trial] now. They [spectators] haven't got any business here no way. What do they come here for? Let them go to the windows and listen.

Perry: All right, sir, does Your Honor deny my motion?

Judge Seabrook: Sure.

Florence explains that there was testimony from Superintendent Gregersen of the Edisto State Park and the arresting officers. Judge Seabrook complained on cross-examination that the defense was asking questions already answered with questioning from the prosecution. "I couldn't believe my ears," she says as she begins to read again.

Judge Seabrook: It's a simple case of trespassing. These people come down here with the purpose, I think, of entering on this State Park . . . although they knew that the law is plainly on the books that they couldn't get in.

Perry: Now, Your Honor, of course you have stated some things that are not in evidence here, and we renew our motion now to have you step aside and disqualify yourself.

Judge Seabrook: I don't believe in all that stuff.

Perry: Well, bear in mind, Your Honor, this is an adversary proceeding, we are trying a case. You have heard the state witness. You have not yet heard from the defendants, but you seem to have made your decision.

Judge Seabrook: Not one bit.

Perry: Is there any further reason for us to . . .

Judge Seabrook: My mind is open. I have been a Magistrate for twenty years. I don't have all this trouble, though. I don't follow up Perry Mason, do you?

"What does a TV show like *Perry Mason* have to do with all of this?" I ask.

"Nothing," Florence says impatiently. "Except it follows the law. And, it didn't get any better. As we expected, the testimony established that the judge was prejudiced or mentally incapacitated. Seabrook made comments like, 'That's all been gone over before by the witnesses for the state.' It was as if he believed there was no reason to let the defendants testify. The lawyers and the witnesses knew what they were doing, but the judge didn't seem able to understand the information given. Finally, Matthew Perry accepted defeat."

Perry: All right, Your Honor, and your decision?

Judge Seabrook: Put them under $50.00 bond, $50.00 bond or thirty days in jail apiece, unless you want to try each one of them separately and I know you are going to appeal.

Perry: Yes, Your Honor. Now Your Honor, let's see, was that a pronouncement of guilt and of your sentence?

Judge Seabrook: Yes, finding them guilty.

Perry: You found them guilty and you placed them under fines of . . .

Judge Seabrook: Fifty dollars apiece, very reasonable . . .

Perry: All right, Your Honor, now we respectfully move the Court for arrest of judgment upon all grounds which we have previously urged at various stages of these proceedings. Does your Honor grant or deny the motion?

Judge Seabrook: Denied . . .

Perry: You are denying them due process in violation of the First and Fourteenth Amendments.

Judge Seabrook: I deny that also. White and colored and then you bring your Fourteenth Amendment to me?

Perry: I understand Your Honor; race is a factor in your ruling, is it not?

Judge Seabrook: Not a bit.

Florence takes a deep breath, looks up at us as we sit incredulous and asks, "Why did I expect anything more? We were warned that we'd lose, but I thought there would at least be some *pretense* of justice."

STATE OF SOUTH CAROLINA)
COUNTY OF CHARLESTON)   IN THE CHARLESTON COUNTY COURT

THE STATE,

-vs-

DENNIS T. BARRETT, LOUIS
BRYANT, JOAN M. KENNEDY,
RAY A. NELSON, DAVID LAWLOR,
JOSEPH FRASIER, CARROLL
SANDERS, GERALDINE GALLASHAW,   ORDER
MARION C. BENNETT, BRUCE L.
MIROFF, JULIA A. TENBRINK,
HENRY WILLIAMS, and HAZEL
M. DANIELS,

        Appellants.

    ON this day came on to be heard the appeal of each of the
Defendants in the foregoing criminal action on the allegations of
errors as set forth in their Notice of Appeal;

    And now, after considering the entire record on file
herein and the arguments of counsel for the Defendants and
for the State, I am of the opinion and it is hereby

    ORDERED that the judgment of the Magistrate's Court
be reversed.

    AND IT IS SO ORDERED.

                _____
                Judge, Charleston County Court

Charleston, South Carolina

October 6th, 1965.

ATTEST: A TRUE COPY
W. LLOYD FLEMING (SEAL)
   CLERK, COUNTY COURT
By Carolyn Welch
    DEPUTY CLERK

By October 6, 1965, the judgment of the Magistrate's Court was overturned.

PASS THE BEDPAN, PLEASE

PINEVILLE
Friday, July 9

It's two days since the stew and just another day of the perpetual dampness that engulfs us here. In our rooms, like most buildings in the Pineville area, we inhale Moldy Eau de Parfum. My envelopes seal themselves before I can use them. Shadows accompany the words in my journal because the ink smudges from the humidity. I slide between clammy sponges at night. I knew I was not going on a vacation when I saw the packing list from SCLC. No electric rollers for a bouffant hairstyle. No fingernail polish or sweet smelling lotions. No cutoffs or short shorts. A different outfit for each activity—no chance. The list included a bare minimum of clothing, so we wear each piece as long as we can stand it. Today Nellie and I draw laundry duty for the pile of dirty clothes collecting in the corner of the loft.

"How are we ever going to wash all of these?" I ask.

Nellie and I look at one another and shake our heads. "By hand," she confirms.

"No choice," I answer, wrinkling my nose. The scavenger hunt begins. What do we wash in? We wander through the guy's bedrooms, walls still stacked high with possessions from past occupants. We try the garbage pit out in the back and the woods nearby. We pile our loot on the ground: one clean chamber pot, a pail and a wash basin. There's no warm water but a leaky hose lies nearby. We spend five cents to get enough Fab to launder clothes and sheets for four voter-registration workers living at Mrs. Martha Simmons's Freedom House.

We set up our assembly line outside on the steps leading up to the girls' loft. "How did we get this job?" I ask using my hands to swish the soap flakes in cold water. We have no heat source, and without heat the water refuses to dissolve the flakes and they form a thick, white scum across the top of the chamber pot.

"Florence and John took the car to Charleston for a meeting with the SCLC leadership," Nellie says. "They're the thinkers. We're the doers." She sorts clothing into piles: underwear, blouses, skirts, dresses, shirts and jeans. (Thank God we only have one man. We can identify our own undies.)

I slide a pair of ladies panties under the scum and say in disgust. "They get covered with a milky film."

"We'll have to be careful when we rinse," she says.

That will be impossible, I think as sweat runs down my arms to join my hands in the sticky water.

"Can you imagine how slaves used to do this?" Nellie comments. "I've heard they boiled, soaked and scrubbed clothes in a mixture with lye."

I wonder aloud, "Every woman in the house wore skirts, blouses, and lots of petticoats."

"And, then there were menstrual rags."

"Ick! And, if no rags, there would be diapers and baby clothes."

"We're lucky, no kids clothes and no bedding. But like them we have sheets and towels—and clothes for at least one man."

"They had hot water, though, even if they did have to collect firewood and keep the fire going."

The afternoon sizzles and threatens rain. Between mixing up "clean" soap batches, we each soak, squeeze, wring, knead and rub garments. The grain of the steps presses into our knees and shins, and our thighs stiffen from kneeling or sitting on our haunches. A hill of clothing grows on a step, slimed with a layer of congealing detergent as the muscles in my hands and forearms cry out for relief. Our attempts at singing freedom songs fizzle. Laundry takes a different sort of inspiration—and perspiration.

Sherie Holbrook on laundry day

"These containers are too small to use to rinse these," Nellie says as she reaches a wet hand up to pull her dark hair out of her eyes.

"Water pressure. We need more water pressure," I whine as water trickles out of the hose. I try to turn it higher. No change.

"Don't complain. At least we have a hose. Slaves had to carry heavy buckets of water."

"Yes, but I bet they had a bigger washtub."

The method becomes obvious. One of us holds each garment while the other runs the hose over it repeatedly attempting to speed the flow with a thumb placed over half the spout. The day drags wearily on.

Surveying the wash festooning the yard, hanging over the picnic table, benches, chairs and the banister we realize our accomplishment has historical perspective.

Before I came to Pineville I occasionally handwashed a sweater or some nylons. Otherwise I used a washing machine without a second thought. Today I realize that we have just participated in a centuries-old process and learned the true price of a clean set of clothes.

THE PROBLEM
WITH HORMONES

PINEVILLE
Saturday, July 10

"What is it in human nature, or at least my nature, that makes me want something when I'm told I can't have it?" I write in my journal the night of my laundry lesson. Take dieting for instance. Normally I willingly eat chocolate cake only on special occasions, but when I decided to lose ten pounds, I swore off any chocolate cake. And, I began to need, want and crave it. Chocolate cake became the proverbial itch that I couldn't scratch.

I itch again and it's not chocolate cake I yearn for. The "punishment" for satisfying this yearning is not gaining a couple of pounds, but possible emotional and physical trauma. Insanely that possible trauma increases the intensity of the itch. The source of *this* yearning: Ishmael Prioleau, Jr., a year and a half younger than I am.

He feels this longing, too. I can see it in his eyes and when he talks, it's usually to me. "How can I be attracted to someone who really isn't here?" I ask myself. Several of the young men in the project come by the Freedom House and hang out during the day. Talking with them is one way we learn about the community. But Ishmael is a dark ghost who appears for a moment or two, watches me and disappears. His lack of presence teases me. I'm conscious that he's not here, come alive when he appears, only to long for him when he vanishes.

An attractive ghost, that's what he is. Tall, dark and handsome. His body has a comfortable athletic look with muscled forearms. Later I will learn that he works long hours in the fields and he takes baseball seriously, hoping to play for the pros. Those brown eyes are sly, like he knows a joke about me he isn't telling. He has a slow smile and beautiful white teeth. His voice is low. His lips are large and, I just know, very soft. I wonder what it would feel like to kiss him. I ask myself if I'll ever find out.

I feel guilty because I'm about to make a mistake. Most southern states have laws against miscegenation, or the interbreeding of people of different races, so I might be considering breaking the law.

We volunteers joked about sexual attraction at orientation in Atlanta, and some SCLC leaders warned us never to date or get caught in a mixed-race pair. Andrew Young did

Ishmael Prioleau's high school graduation picture

say something like we know you are kids in the prime of your sexual lives. We know things may happen. Be discreet. Your lives may depend upon it.

We had no inkling where temptation might come from in the communities we entered or if the warnings were even necessary. But they were. I remember Florence's astonished report.

"You'd never believe what happened to me today," she said a day or two after we arrived in Pineville. "A Negro in a pickup stopped as I was walking across the parking lot." She shook her head in disbelief. "He wanted to know if I would marry him."

And I remember talking to Julie in early July.

"Remember that Bob on the SCOPE team?" she asked me.

"Of course," I said. "He was the one who told us that we were out of money. Disrespectful. That's the way he treated Florence."

"Well, he proposed to me."

I said, "What!" Two wedding proposals in a month is something we didn't expect.

Now I don't think these proposals were about marriage. I wonder if they are laughing at us or if these are serious sexual invitations. But they do point out the difficulty of our situation. We are four white strangers in a Negro world. Very few young women in Pineville are allowed to work with us because of the danger, but young men come to find out what our project is about and to learn about us—and three of us are female. I realize one of the reasons the local guys come to work for us is to check out the white girls. What do white girls smell like, talk like, and think about?

I'm eighteen, single and just as curious about how *they* think, talk and smell. Some of the guys don't talk much, they just stare. Others are comfortable talking about registering voters and hanging out.

Ishmael hasn't had the talk from orientation and he doesn't seem to care what the Pineville community will think about us. But I have and I definitely do. Besides, I'm not living in the perfect dating situation. I haven't had a real bath since we left Atlanta—just hasty wash-ups with the hose in the open space behind the store. My clothes get washed but they always smell musty and funky because they never dry. I didn't bring a razor and I swear my deodorant barely works in this humid heat. My hair hangs wearily and most of the time I don't even try to put on makeup, because it just sort of melts into a smudge. When I get home at the end of the summer my father will tell me my skin looks like a Guatemalan countryside: bumpy and pitted. I hardly feel like a sexy California girl. Flirting is part of California culture, the long blond hair, the bikini on the beach and the "necking" at the drive-in. But that's in California and even there, it's not me.

And we're not in California. Ishmael lives two blocks away, but for the first two weeks he didn't hang out at the Freedom House like some of the kids. By mid-July he has become more comfortable at the Freedom House, staying for a couple of hours at a time. Physically he can't be missed, but he is so quiet he rarely speaks. Nellie thinks he's sullen. I think he's shy.

I'm sitting at the picnic table behind the store one afternoon writing a report.

"Will you 'go with me' tonight?" Ishmael whispers leaning over me before he sits.

"Sitting at this table is the only place *we're* going," I answer, totally missing the intent of the question. "Do you plan to be a minister like your father?"

"Only if Ah'm called by the Holy Spirit," he answers, accepting the new subject. "Preachin' isn't what Ah want to do. Ah want to play baseball for the L.A. Dodgers."

"That's my mom and dad's team," I answer. "So, why don't you just decide not to be a preacher?"

"Ah'm afraid of what God will do if He calls an' Ah refuse to follow His call. My daddy refused three times before the Lord convinced him he *wanted* to be pastor at Day Dawn Baptist Church."

"So, you believe in a God of fear," I comment, shaking my head and thinking to myself that I believe in a God of love.

"Ah believe in a God that knows what Ah should do with my life," he replies.

Ishmael begins canvassing the community for voters and is at the store more frequently. At the table on another evening he runs his finger down my arm and asks, "Will you 'go with me' tonight?"

"Where can we go?" I ask. "We can't go to the movie or a cafe in St. Stephen together. School activities are out for the summer and I'm not sure I could go to your school anyway."

"But Ah want you to." This time he changes the subject. "How many children do you plan to have?" he asks.

"Are you crazy?" I say. "Ishmael, why would I want to bring babies into a world as ugly as the one we live in?"

"You don't want children?" It's the first time he looks like I might not be the girl for him.

"No, I don't."

This time it's Ishmael who shakes his head. "But God put us here to have children."

"If God wants me to have children, he needs to create a world that is nurturing and kind. Not one where you and I are taking a chance just talking to one another. America is no place to raise children."

"Ah think you're making a mistake," he says, standing up. He puts his arm around my shoulder and whispers in my ear, "You'll be sorry. See you tomorrow." And he walks away. It takes a full minute for my heart to quit thumping in my chest, and I wonder if the mistake is about not having children or not going with him.

"There's a house party in Cross tonight. Come with me," Ishmael says walking into the store one morning three days later.

"You know I can't," I reply. I enjoy the banter and the challenge. I'm flirting a little, I know.

"Let's check with Mrs. Simmons and see what she says."

"She'll say no." But she doesn't say no. She feels we'd be safe on the ten or so miles of road between Pineville and the small town of Cross to the southwest. So, I say yes. And wonder immediately if I should have.

When Ishmael arrives in his father's car, Mae and I are waiting for him, actually giggling about my "date." He slips a piece of paper into my hand, and I put it in my pack, without reading it.

"Ishmael, can we take Mae to Maxine's?" I ask. Most folks don't have cars, so it's usual to give people a ride if they are going in your direction.

He gestures us both into the car and we're on our way. Mae and I chatter as Ishmael drives silently.

"Come on in," Mae says to us both. I get out and start for Maxine's house before I realize Ishmael hasn't opened his door.

"I'll be right back," I call to him as I disappear into the house.

Fifteen minutes later I feel guilty that Ishmael is still in the car. When I open the front door to leave, I see a second car with its lights on parked next to Ishmael's. A tall, blond man is talking with Ishmael through the window. I go stone cold and frozen on the step until the man stands up and I realize it's John, not some Klansman.

He turns on me as I approach the car.

"What are you doing riding alone with Ishmael?" he demands. "You know it's dangerous."

"Mae was with us until we got here," I protest, controlling my voice, which sounds remarkably like I've been chastised by my father. "Besides, Mrs. Simmons said it would be safe for us to go to Cross together."

"I don't care what Mrs. Simmons said. You are *never* to be alone in a car with a Negro man." He turns back to Ishmael angrily, "And what are you thinking of?"

"Ah had Sherie check with Mrs. Simmons before Ah carried her here," Ishmael says, his voice even softer than usual, barely a whisper.

"You two are going to do what you want to do. So go on and do it,"

John says as he stomps back to his car and drives away. After John leaves I go to the passenger door, too embarrassed to open it. When I finally get up the nerve, the atmosphere in the car chills us as we drive. I don't think we know what to say to one another. Neither of us has been in this position before. We've done nothing wrong except being Negro and white. It's a long fifteen minutes until we near Cross.

Loud and crowded, the house party grates on our already strained nerves. Local teenagers jostle against one another until they see us and then they stare. One young man asks, "Is y'all from 'round here? Is y'all married?"

"What's that white girl doin' here?" someone yells from the doorway.

Rather than become the entertainment, we step outside and walk down a path away from the pavement where we won't be seen.

"This evening has been a lesson," I start the conversation. Ishmael takes my hand as we walk. "If we see each other, it will always be like this."

He doesn't reply.

"What were you thinking of when you asked me out?" I ask hesitantly.

"Ah've never dated a girl like you before," he says, being careful not to mention that I'm white.

We walk on quietly but comfortably. I feel the damp of the swamp and mosquitoes swarm around my legs and arms. Tomorrow morning I will count seventy-five mosquito bites on my left leg alone, but tonight I'm just glad to be here alone with him and I let the skeeters taste my blood.

"What do you want to do after you graduate from Russellville High?" I ask.

"Ah'd like to go to Allen or Benedict an' study mathematics," he answers.

"And play pro ball."

"Yaas."

"There aren't a lot options for entertainment in the country," I continue. "What do you do on a first date?" I ask before I realize it might be a risky question.

He stops and turns to face me. He smiles broadly and answers, "I can' tell you that." He bends down to kiss me. I respond to his soft lips and his exciting arms around me. How can something that feels so right . . . But, we aren't supposed to do this and I wonder why I came. It was irresponsible. Although he's more than a year younger, I like this man, but I'm old-fashioned. I don't believe in sex before marriage and the fact that he is forbidden fruit does not cancel that value.

I move away and begin walking again.

"Go with me tonight," he says, grasping my arm and pulling me to him. It isn't a question as it has been before and his voice is demanding. Finally I get the message that he's talking about sex.

"No. I can't," I answer, stepping away again. "I think you better take me home."

"But Ah can make you happier than you've ever bin. Did you read the poem Ah wrote for you?" He doesn't reach for me but I start back for the car anyway, remembering the paper in my pack. I will find later that it is a love poem.

"I've let this go too far," I say. "I don't believe in anything but kissing before marriage."

Ishmael catches me and grabs my shoulder to stop me.

"You don't mean that. You want me," he says softly and he's right, but I'm not kidding or making conversation. I meant what I said.

"I want to go home. I like to kiss you, but that's as far as I want to go."

"You'd do it in California," he persists.

"Absolutely not," I say. "I don't 'do it' in California. I kiss or hug someone I'm interested in, but that's all." What seemed like a romantic evening is losing its glitter. It's becoming awkward.

"It's not that way here," he says as he turns me toward the car. "We don't kiss a girl because we like her. A kiss is an invitation to go to bed even on a first date."

"Not this time, Ishmael. I can't." I feel nervous for the first time and unsure of him. I won't go with him, but the temptation is still strong.

"In time you will," he says and I can see his smile in the lights from the house. He is so sure of himself. I accept the challenge in my mind but my body is definitely disappointed.

A LINE IN THE SAND: CANVASSING

PINEVILLE
Wednesday, July 14

Almost a week after laundry day, I'm out canvassing again, alone this time. I look at the next name on my list and glance up at the little house beside the dirt road. I wonder who lives in this house with a big dooryard surrounded by pines.

Blue. Once the paint was blue. Weathered, sun-tarnished, the house slumps on the sand in the clearing. The door stands open and though the few windows are glass free, it's dark inside. A rusty tin roof shades the front porch and steps. A shabby cane chair, a broken box of firewood, that's all there is.

The woman is as weathered as her home, dressed in a grey skirt and a darker grey blouse. Her hair, black and gray, is pulled severely back from her sienna face. Her skirt stops at cracked, bare feet as she stands on the hot sand and watches me trudge up the road.

The grit of the lane pulls at my low-heeled white pumps, making each step a commitment and the runs in my nylons and scratches on my legs bear witness to an earlier encounter with a blackberry bush. The clouds form a lid on the pot of humidity I've simmered in since June. Sweat oozes persistently between my breasts, under my arms, down my

Many miles of sandy, dusty roads lead between fields to concealed cabins.

thighs and my hair sags against my neck for support. Many hand wash-ings have not released the moldy whisper from my orange-and-yellow striped cotton dress, which glues itself to my damp body. I yearn to be dry.

What is she thinking as she watches me? White folks drive up in cars; they don't walk up to the house. I surmise she goes to church regu-larly because everyone here does. She probably guesses I'm a civil rights worker. When I reach her, her eyes are veiled, but not cold. She doesn't trust me, but she isn't locking me out.

"Evenin'," I say politely, following local custom, although it's just past noon. "Mrs. Crawford?"

"Evenin'," she answers, her voice almost a whisper as she studies her feet. She isn't going to help me.

"My name is Sherie Holbrook and I'm here registering voters for Dr. Martin Luther King, Jr."

Rebecca Crawford and Gregory Sumpter

At the magic words—Dr. Martin Luther King, Jr.—she looks up at me quickly and then down.

"We're talking to people about going to the courthouse to register to vote. Have you registered yet?" I wish she would offer me a glass of water.

The soft voice answers, "Yaas, ma'am." Perhaps I will go away now.

I don't believe her, but just as I had been taught, I say exuberantly, "Good for you, so few people have. Do you have your registration card?"

"Yaas, ma'am." She turns toward the house, limping slightly as she walks up the steps and disappears into the darkness. Time goes by. I think she has decided not to return. Sometimes, that's what folks do. They just disappear so they won't have to explain they are terrified to vote.

And here I am bringing danger right onto her front porch. Mrs. Crawford has no job and her husband died long ago. She has no children who can be hurt, because they moved away for jobs in the cities. But she has this shabby little house and she knows it can easily be burned to the ground.

When she reappears, her hands are empty except for calluses. "Can' find it," she mumbles an apology.

"But you don't need it." I don't want her to get away. "You can help us anyway because you have registered to vote." She glances up at me for a second, gauging my credibility.

"On next Monday, we're taking a busload of people down to Moncks Corner to register. If you come with us, you can help them understand how important voting is and they will see that you've done it."

"Yaas, ma'am," she murmurs. "I'll come."

"We're meeting at Redeemer Church at ten," I say.

"Yaas, ma'am."

I turn and trudge away, sure she will be too frightened to get on the bus to vote. She is another one of hundreds of people I'll talk to about voting this summer and most will turn down my invitation.

A LINE IN THE SAND:
REGISTRATION DAY

PINEVILLE
Monday, July 19

I'm vaguely disappointed, but not surprised that Mrs. Crawford is not there as the old, faded-green bus arrives at the church parking lot and rests before the crowd of quiet people. The importance of registering to vote is emphasized this sultry morning by their attire: Sunday dresses and suits, fancy hats with feathers and tulle, polished shoes, pocketbooks. They are too quiet, too afraid, but they are here. They deserve more. They deserve to celebrate their courage! Florence, our project leader, begins to sing an old spiritual. "Oh, Freedom. Oh, Freedom. Oh, Freedom over me. And before I'd be a slave, I'd be buried in my grave and go home to my Lord and be free." The crowd tentatively follows her lead.

The civil rights workers step up the tempo by singing "Keep Your Eyes on the Prize." Voices commit more in volume and conviction. With "Ain't Gonna Let Nobody Turn Me Round," the crowd picks up the verse and their pride as everyone gets on the bus and it slowly winds out onto the road.

Inside the bus, fans flutter like butterflies to beat back the heat. Many have pictures of Dr. Martin Luther King, Jr. on them, others bear the image of Jesus. Someone else sees her first, walking slowly toward the church, waving her handkerchief. The bus creaks to a stop and Mrs. Crawford climbs aboard.

She comes down the aisle, settles into the empty seat next to me and smiles as she meets my eyes. A white straw hat, patent-leather purse and shoes spruce up a light-green dress.

"Everyone!" I announce. "Mrs. Crawford has already registered to vote and she has come to answer your questions about doing it." Applause and we go on singing.

She sits quietly next to me in her broad-brimmed straw hat. Five miles go by, and then she whispers, "Chile, Ah ain't never register."

I whisper back, "You will today."

"Ah can' read or write."

"I'll teach you. You just need to sign your name."

"Ah can'."

"We have time. I'll show you."

I take a pencil from my purse and turn to the back of the map of Berkeley County. I slowly write *Rebecca Crawford.* I can tell it's just too much as a furrow tightens between her eyes and her gaze drops to her lap.

"Wait. Let's start one letter at a time. Here, write over the top of this letter R." I write the R and hand her the pencil and paper. Awkwardly, she traces the letter over and over. "Now, write the **R** fresh here below." Her hand shakes as she tries. I can't recognize the letter and we start again.

Fifteen miles is not very far when you're trying to overcome 250 years of defeat. Painstakingly we make sure each of our people knows where to sign their registration form. We register 150 people in Moncks Corner this day, without fanfare under the watchful eyes of the white registration staff. But Rebecca Crawford is not one of them.

I'm torn. Although Mrs. Crawford doesn't seem disappointed, I'm despondent. But I'm also proud. We've done what we came here to do: register voters.

On the bus going home, a determined Mrs. Crawford asks me to come and teach her, so she can register next time. I promise I will. I have nothing to give her with her name on it when I retrieve the map as we bump back into Redeemer's parking lot. I expect her to be saddened by her failure, but she smiles at me and reminds me, "Ya come back for sure an' learn me what Ah needs to know."

Florence and Nellie are buoyant—our first registration day was a success. I know I should be jubilant, but Mrs. Crawford has touched my heart. I feel like I let her down.

There is a surprise waiting for us when we walk into the Freedom House. His name: Louis "Lefty" Bryant. Bob and Negro George said they would send someone to help us. Lefty is that someone. Negro and a Movement veteran, he's in his early twenties, arrested more than twenty times. He is the charismatic leader we need. He's also cocky and opinionated and a specialist in direct action. I do believe things will be different around here.

(l to r) Deke White, Louis Bryant, Herbert Mitchell and James Summers

THE PROBLEM WITH
HORMONES: PROBLEM SOLVED

PINEVILLE
Friday, July 31

"We're planning to send you back to Charleston," John says about two weeks later, his eyes hard and face stoic. It's early evening and I'm sitting at the back of the Freedom House writing a letter to my mother when he approaches.

I'm dumbfounded. "Charleston! Why?" I catch my breath. I don't want to work in Charleston.

"Because your relationship with Ishmael is endangering this project."

My shock turns to anger. I am guilty of flirting with Ishmael, but we have done nothing more. I am an adult (though just by a few months) and I don't think I deserve to be talked to this way.

"What relationship?" I demand. My hands are hot and I want to slap his impassive face.

"You flirt with him. You act like you did in Atlanta and I've already talked to you about that."

Oh, yes, I remember that conversation. This is not the first time John has commented on my behavior. In late June, John and I spent one evening together while the rest were at church. One of his first remarks was that I had been flirtatious in Atlanta. He based his accusation on the fact that he had seen me leave the gym with a fellow wearing a goatee. The young man had his arm around me. What young man? I told him I hadn't met anyone with a goatee at orientation. And I hadn't.

"Charleston is big enough you could probably get away with seeing a Negro," John finishes and walks away. I'm left sitting there, pen in hand, feeling accused of something I haven't done. My reason for enjoying Ishmael is not because he's a Negro. It's because we actually have learned enough about one another to feel close.

Apparently John is here to save me from myself. He turns back to me sitting at the table and says, "I've written a letter to SCLC/NAACP in Charleston, but I haven't mailed it yet."

You think threatening me will save you the trouble, I think to myself. Later I learn he may not have sent the letter, but he did talk to the civil rights workers on the Charleston project. They expect me to be moving in there. I don't comment. Apparently he isn't done.

"Florence agrees with me that you have a problem." I know my face is red and there are tears in my eyes, but I don't respond.

"She's going to talk to the older people here in the community to see if you and Ishmael are a problem for them. If so, I'll mail the letter." This time he walks away without turning back.

I have nothing to say because he obviously does not want to listen to me.

The next day I write in my journal: "I wonder if I really am any good down here. I realize what my selfishness with Ishmael could have done to the project. I've acted like a love-struck kid. Perhaps I deserve to return to Charleston."

I promise myself I will go nowhere with Ishmael unless someone else is with us and we are taking care of the business I came down here for. I hope it's not too late. I will keep my promise.

IN GOD'S HANDS

PINEVILLE
Sunday, August 8

It's been two weeks since that first registration day and on Monday, August 2, we register 200 new voters. Under Lefty's direction, we've also begun to confront local businesses about their segregation policies. Our youth group attempts to eat at Bennett's Restaurant in St. Stephen, but we're turned away at gunpoint. We also try to get into the Star Theater in St. Stephen. Negroes are only allowed to sit in the balcony, not on the main floor. The theater closes rather than desegregate. Six white cars with Klansmen drive past the Freedom House every week or so with Confederate flags flying.

We go to bed each night almost too exhausted to sleep.

"Fire! Fire at J.K.!" John's voice yells to alert us all. It's after 11:00 p.m. and we waken to the overpowering smell of smoke from J.K. Gourdin Elementary School two blocks away.[1] From the store parking lot we can see a menacing red smudge in the brick administration office windows.

"We gotta stop it ourselves," a local volunteer yells. "The damn white fire department in St. Stephen won't do shit."

"Grab pots from the kitchen," John shouts, seizing our only bucket from the yard. "Sherie, wake up Mrs. Simmons and have her call the fire department, anyway."

I race for the house. At the hose bib John directs, "Don't fill it too full or you'll just spill it." Water sloshes onto the pavement, leaving a trail to evaporate uselessly into the air. By the time I throw a trickle of water on the fire from a saucepan, cars full of white men are parked on the road watching our attempts to save the school. The flames engulf the office and book room.

"Where the hell did that come from?" a Negro voice cries out as a red fire engine rolls up ten minutes later with the promise of help in the silver tank on the back. We applaud. Before the truck, we were the school's only defenders. We're in farm country and there are no hydrants. The water tank holds relief as firemen jump out and run hoses toward the flames.

A fireman yells, "Stay back, niggahs!" Then he laughs and we learn the truth. The large silver tank is empty.

"Those assholes. They deliberately came empty," John swears, his face smeared with sweat and ashes. "Well, they warned us. If we stay, this whole town is on its own." He throws his bucket against the ground in disgust and anger. The firemen laugh at us as they roll up the hoses and a cortege of cars follows the engine back toward St. Stephen. We survey the ruins of the administration building and textbook storage room, both completely gutted. We have caused this.

---

1. "Once the Berkeley School System was established after 1920 . . . Pineville's black community took advantage of the state's promise of $1 per student per year and established their own schools." One was at Redeemer Episcopal Church. "In the early 1920s, J.K. Gourdin, one of the patriarchs of white Gourdin and Marion families who had resettled Pineville after Reconstruction, saw a need for a public school for black children in the community. He swapped land with the black Gourdine and Brown families to create a large plot at the junction of Highway 45 and Russellville Road. He then gave the land for the school and assisted in building it in 1925, which was named the J.K. Gourdin School." Montgomery, Warner M., "Pineville, A Historic Refuge," *The Columbia Star*. Jan. 18, 2008. <http://www.thecolumbiastar.com/news/2008-01-18/travel/034.html>.

J.K. Gourdin Elementary School the day after the fire

The following Sunday, at Redeemer Church, the sermon demands love for the white folks who would destroy a school. Unlike church services at home where the minister gives a sermon, there's a give-and-take with the congregation that I'm growing used to.

Rev. Gadsden calls, "*Somebody* broke the window of *that* room!"

"Yaas, sir," the seated congregation responds, rocking from side to side.

"Ah say, *somebody* threw *gas* on the floor of *that* room," his voice strengthens.

"Tha's right." The swaying continues.

"*Somebody* threw a *match* on that *floor*," he exhorts them.

"Yaas, Lord."

Back and forth it goes, the voices creating a musical chorus of determination and unity.

"Part of the school is gone. We can' bring it back."

"No, sir."

"What do we got to do?" he demands.

No answer, just a wave of fluttering fans.

"What do we got to do?" he asks again.

Hands clap; faces are riveted on him.

"What do we got to do?" He hesitates at the peak. "We got to love them."

"Tha's right."

"We got to love an' forgive 'em," his voice a little softer.

"Thank you, Jesus."

"Tha's right. We got to love an' forgive them."

"Thank you, Lord."

Rev. Gadsden wipes his forehead with a handkerchief. Those of us who were at the fire are sitting together. We look at one another in utter amazement. Love and forgive.

As in the past, the people call on the Lord to sustain them through the hard times and they sing the words of "Amazing Grace:"

Through many dangers, toils and snares
we have already come
T'was grace that brought us safe thus far
and grace will lead us home.

This picture of Redeemer Reformed Episcopal Church, Pineville, S. C. was taken in February, 1965. The building seated 700 people and was the largest church building in Berkeley County, South Carolina.

They settle in and patiently await the next catastrophe. Pray for these white folks! Love them! At orientation that made sense. But here and now I don't understand. In time, I will experience their resignation and trust in the Lord often enough for it to become a part of me. Now, however, I want to explode with anger.

But I can't. I want to break something, throw something, yell something, but I can't. Stoic, is that the word? My parents raised me to deal with anger rationally and coolly, never losing control. And so, I turn the anger inward and I ask myself about God. How could the loving God I believed in allow such pain to afflict a people who love him deeply and try daily to live by His law? And then I consider the congregation of Redeemer and my anger feels rightly placed in God's hands.

United Klans Of America, Inc.

KNIGHTS OF THE
KU KLUX KLAN

WILL PRESENT A PROGRAM

1965

Sunday Evening, August 1
7:00 P. M.
St. Stephens, S. C.

1½ Miles East Of St. Stephens On Highway 45

Come Hear The Truth
Several Good Speakers
The White Public Is Invited

Authorized By The Board Of Directors The United Klans Of America, Inc.
National Office: Suite 401, Alston Building, Tuscaloosa, Alabama
S. C. Office: Box 4144, Spartanburg, S. C.
Sponsored by the South Carolina State Office and St. Stephens Lodge No. 22

WE DON'T
SERVE COLORED HERE: TEST

MONCKS CORNER
Tuesday, August 17

Nine days after the school fire we aren't surprised when Mr. Howard throws us out of his cafe. This is our first visit as a group of both Negroes and whites attempting to eat at his segregated restaurant. I say it was the first visit because the nine of us are only there to determine if Howard's serves out-of-state customers and if he serves Negroes. We chose the lunchroom on the main street in Moncks Corner, because it sits near the train depot and offers a nice place to eat for out-of-state travelers.

Pat (who is white) goes in first and sits at the counter. We see the waitress chat briefly and know Pat is mentioning she's from California while she orders a cup of coffee.

Through the picture window we see her served. Six Negro workers, Florence and I go in and sit at the counter next to Pat.

"We don't serve niggah lovers here," the waitress hisses when we order coffee.

Lefty calls for coffee from a table in the corner where the Negro workers sit, waiting patiently.

The waitress spits, "We don't serve colored here." She lifts the phone and mutters, "There are a lot of *them* here." Then she turns back to us.

The Pineville SCOPE project meets members of the Ku Klux Klan in front of Howard's Restaurant.

"We're closed," she announces. "Y'all have to go." The other white customers hastily lay money on the tables and leave.

The owner hustles in the front door, tightlipped and deliberate. "This restaurant is closed. Get the hell out!"

"The Congress of the United States just passed a law saying we can stay. You don't sound very happy with Washington," Florence responds.

"You're damn right. Get the hell out!"

My legs wobble a bit getting off the stool and I pray I make it to the door before they give out.

We return the next day and Mr. Howard locks the door. The eight of us form a picket line walking back and forth on the sidewalk singing freedom songs. Time drags along as the heat rises in waves from the sidewalk.

At lunchtime some customers turn away quickly when they see us. Others reach for the doorknob and find it locked. They stare at us; some snarl "niggah" and "bitch."

As I cross the street to take pictures, a yellow Ford Fairlane, Confederate flag adorning the antenna, prowls by with a white man and six teenage boys. My heart nearly stops when he parks at the curb just past the restaurant and two more cars of white men park behind him so our group is sandwiched between the cars and the restaurant. Men leave their cars and stand blocking our path. Lefty orders, "Mae and Maxine, go on down the street a few doors." Lefty, Kenny (a high school student Lefty recruited locally) and Bobby turn to face the white men.

"Niggahs! Get off the sidewalk! If you wants to waste your time walkin', walk in the damn street. Fuckin' niggah bastards deserve to die." Pointing at me across the street he yelled, "Martin Luther King is only one communist in a bunch of niggah communists." To me he says, "Bitch! Why don't you go back to Russia?"

Two policemen step out of their cruiser and unenthusiastically approach the man.

"Alden*, what you doin'?" one asks.

"Bert*, these niggahs and that bitch are blockin' the sidewalk! Arrest them or we'll get rid of 'em."

"Alden, what they're doin' is legal. I cain't arrest 'em," Bert explains quietly.

After a tense standoff, a second police car arrives and folks begin to leave until there are only a few left on the street. Warily we keep walking. When the street mostly clears, Lefty tells the local Negro folks we'll be back.

"Join us!" he urges. "These crackers can' keep us from gettin' our freedom."

I crank up the Pontiac. Pleased, we leave Moncks Corner singing "Oh Freedom."

As I drive out of town I concentrate to obey the speed limit. We don't want to give them a single reason to arrest us as our voices rise in celebration.

---

* Alden and Bert are fictitious names.

GO AWAY SO NOBODY KNOWS

"Here they come!" Kenny exclaims from the backseat of the station wagon ten minutes after we leave Howard's Restaurant in Moncks Corner. "Here they come!" I grip the steering wheel tighter and watch the rearview mirror. We're driving through a sparsely settled stretch of piney woods between Moncks Corner and Pineville.

Bam! The yellow Fairlane with the Confederate flag hits our back bumper! One of the girls screams. I jam the gas pedal to the floor, but they smack us again, then again.

"Hit the gas, Sherie!"

"No! Hit the brake!"

A black '56 Chevy shoots out from behind the Fairlane, roars past and then swerves in front of us and comes almost to a full stop. I slam on the brakes. Then I hit the gas to avoid the Fairlaine behind. Inside, my passengers are hurled forward then jerked back.

Lefty yells, "Don't let them box us in!" I gun the motor to pass the Chevy on the left, but the driver hits the gas and pulls in front of me. I drop back behind him and jam on the brakes. Just ahead the road arches over the train tracks one hundred feet below. There are no guardrails.

"God, what do I do?" Defensive driving was not part of our orientation in Atlanta. Everyone yells advice at me, and finally Lefty screams over the din that I should pass on the right. Gritting my teeth, I swerve off the pavement onto the shoulder, but have to brake immediately for the Chevy, which has anticipated my move.

I jolt back onto the asphalt. Our car quivers and dies! I frantically twist the key in the ignition. It won't crank and we sit in sudden, dazed silence. Lefty's voice begins, "We Shall Not Be Moved."

"We're fightin' for our freedom, we shall not be moved."

Voices behind me join in, "We're fightin' for our freedom, we shall not be moved."

Resigned, I join them, "Just like a tree tha's standin' by the water, we shall not be moved." Our singing is part bravado, part desperation and part determination.

Laughing, the white men leave their cars and swagger around our car pounding on the hood, windows and top. Hastily I roll up my window, but I should have locked the door first. A white boy jerks it open. I yank it back with sheer adrenaline and lock it.

Fear overcomes us and we fall silent, except for Lefty, who continues singing, deliberately taunting our attackers. He sits in front and to our horror, one of the white men swings a wrench, shattering the passenger window. He grabs Lefty by the throat. Lefty flails about in an attempt to break free. I grab him and hold him against my shoulder, sprawled over the top of the girl squeezed between us. Maxine grabs Lefty's arm from the backseat and I remind them to be nonviolent. Lefty croaks, "Let's get out!"

But Maxine and I hold Lefty tight; my hands are under his arm and over his chest. I feel his shirt tearing as they try to pull him out of the car.

The chaos inside the car is total. Bobby keeps shouting, "Let me get out an' fight!" But he's hemmed in by other bodies. We beg everyone to be nonviolent. It's mid-afternoon and though this is a highway, few cars go by. People passing in cars— white people—just stare and keep driving. Negroes look away and speed up.

A man shatters a back window and forces the door open. Mae and one of the other local workers hold Kenny to keep him from fighting and to keep the men from pulling him out. The men take turns beating him about the head.

Exhausted, Lefty is finally dragged from the car. Experienced and now under control, he becomes limp and nonviolent. Kenny's assailants abandon him to join the assault on Lefty, fists pummeling and feet kicking until he falls to the ground.

Chortling and hooting, the men from the Chevy lounge against its fender, light cigarettes and watch us. Lefty staggers to his feet. Disoriented and angry he picks up a bottle from the side of the road and lurches toward the Chevy. The driver revs his engine and drives right at Lefty, but Bobby tackles him and yanks him to safety. The driver halts, reaches back and points a shotgun out the window. He coaxes, "Please niggah, come closer." Lefty slumps on the side of the road. We hurry toward him, ignoring the Chevy as it turns toward town.

The rural highway is empty, but we are not alone. As we survey our situation we realize an elderly white lady with silver hair has been watching the terrifying situation. She must know we are desperate and frightened, because she steps off of her porch and beckons to me.

I approach and she says, "I'm so sorry, honey, about what those men did. I wanted to help, but I live so close to the road. The Klan could burn my house so fast. Do you need to make a phone call? That's all I can do—let you use my phone. Then go away so no one knows you were here."

And that's what I do. I'm shaking so hard, I nearly drop the phone as I call the Freedom House. Nellie is there alone, without a car, so we're on our own.

I manage to stammer a thank-you to the old woman, but my hand

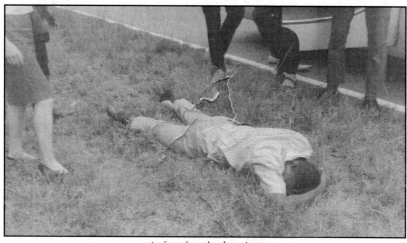

Lefty after the beating

misses the doorknob twice before I'm able to grasp it. This is what we'd seen on television and, for the first time, violence has been directed at us individually. Adrenaline charges and unbalances my gait. I'm afraid. Afraid I'll be sick. Afraid for Lefty.

When I reach the car, Lefty is sitting with his back against the front tire, eyes open but glazed over. The other passengers surround him and Maxine asks him questions.

"Where ya hurt?"

"All over," he answers hoarsely.

"Lefty, move yor arms an' legs."

He raises his hand to touch a cut on his forehead.

"How's ya breathin'?"

"Girl, Ah ain't dead. Ah jus' got beat. Ah bin beat befo'. Ah be fine as soons Ah can get to Mrs. Simmons's." He struggles to his feet.

"I hope we can do that," I say grimly, walking to the driver's door. I brush broken glass off the seat, nicking my palm, and find the key in the ignition where I'd left it. My blood trickles onto my dress and I start to cry, my face against the steering wheel. From somewhere in the backseat I feel a comforting hand on my shoulder and I realize all eight of us are back in the car.

I turn the key and nothing happens. I try again. Nothing. Someone says, "Be careful not to flood it," and I realize that far from flooding it, I haven't been giving it gas.

Praying there's a way home, I turn the key and step on the accelerator. The Pontiac purrs like we just drove off the sales lot; I put the car in gear and pull slowly away. We deflate and crumple in our seats. Then quietly from Lefty we hear,

> *"We shall overcome.*
> *We shall overcome.*
> *We shall overcome some day."*

We join in as we drive somberly back to the Freedom House. My stomach settles, my heartbeat slowly approaches normal. But my brain races. I'm no longer afraid, but I'm not triumphant either. Numb is all I feel. We survived, but will we be so lucky next time? I just want to get home.

SO MUCH
FOR THE HIPPOCRATIC OATH

Twenty-five minutes later, we're home at the Freedom House, but it doesn't feel safe anymore. When we drive into the parking lot, I see Herb helping Florence out of the back of a car. She and Pat took three local workers, Herb, Azell and Henry, to the Berkeley Restaurant in Moncks Corner while we were at Howard's. Florence limps toward the picnic table and her hair is a tangled mess.

Nellie hurries up to Lefty's door. "Are you all right?" she says, stepping back from the broken glass that falls out of the window when he opens it.

"Yaas," he answers. "What happened to Florence?"

"They got inside the Berkeley Restaurant. That's all I know. She said they'll tell us as soon as you get settled."

"If one of us getting cut up means we're really civil rights workers, we've arrived," Florence says shakily, swinging her leg over the bench to sit at the table, being careful not to put any pressure on a large bandage on her calf. Band-Aids bedeck her face and arms. "Would someone please get me a soda? I'm so dry."

"Are you all alright?" I ask Azell, Herb and Henry.

"Yeah, we're knocked around, but we're fine. It's Florence needed to go to the hospital," Herb answers.

"What happened?" Lefty demands. In their concern over Florence, no one notices the bruises on Lefty and Kenny or the broken windows in the Pontiac.

"A couple customers didn't want to share sandwiches, salads and iced teas with us," Azell says as Henry returns with a grape Nehi. Lefty starts to interrupt, but lets the story unfold.

"We were surprised the people at the Berkeley Restaurant let us walk in an' sit down like normal customers," Herb begins. "Then we waited. We tied up two tables near the door an' Ah think they decided they would just wait us out. The place was full, so they had lots of customers."

Florence takes up the story. "Suddenly a huge fat man threw his fork down on his plate and threatened, 'I'll have you niggahs for dessert!' He slammed his chair back, stood up and everyone watched as he came toward us. I mean that place went silent. Herb was closest to the door. The fat man wrapped his right arm around Herb's neck, hoisted him out of his seat and pushed him right out the open door."

"Then he grabbed me by the hair," Pat says. "He drug me across two chairs and shoved me out the door and down the steps."

"Ah'd had enough," Azell says. "Ah tried to get to the door but the fat man punched me in the side of the head as Ah passed him."

"The next thing I knew," Pat says, "here's Azell crashing into me as I tried to stand up."

Florence continues, "There was a table between Henry and the door, but the big one reached right over it. He was dragging Henry across the table but he lost his grip and Henry ended up on the floor. The guy grabbed him again and threw him out. He was just so strong. Another customer slammed the door shut.

"I was sitting at the counter and the two of them each grabbed an arm and jerked me off the stool. I remembered to go limp, but they dragged me to the door. I'm not a small woman.

Nellie and two of the Snipe girls in front of the Freedom House the day of a Klan drive-by. The sign across the gas pumps says, "We Shall Overcome."

Bennett's Restaurant changed to Bennett's Private Club to avoid desegregating.

I couldn't believe it when the big man lifted me up and threw me right through the glass door onto the sidewalk."

"Then," says Herb, "this little guy came out. A white guy. He stood on the top step, shook his finger at us and said, 'You're all a bunch of fuckin' communists, but she's bleedin'. Git in my truck and I'll carry her to the hospital.' He walked over to a red pickup parked at the curb, but we just stared at him," Herb added. "We didn't hardly dare trust him, but we didn't have much choice. Florence was bleeding enough to scare us all."

Pat says they got Florence up in the back of the truck and tried to stop the bleeding with a bunch of paper napkins, but Florence's face was so pale they were all very scared. In less than five minutes they were at the back door of the hospital and Pat helped Florence inside.

"So, there I am," says Florence, "bleeding all over the place and the receptionist—an old prune of a white woman—asked me what happened." Then she said, 'Y'all are in the wrong place. Whites don't come into the colored wing.'

"I told her I'd been thrown through the door at the Berkeley Restaurant because I was with Negro customers. She looked like she'd stepped in dog shit, but she took us down the hall to an examination room."

"But nothing happened," Pat says indignantly. "And she's still bleeding like crazy. I tried to stop it with a box of Kleenex on the counter, but it didn't take long to use it all up."

"Finally," Florence says, reaching down to press the end of some tape against her leg more securely, "this white doctor arrives. The only thing he said was to call me a bitch while he looked at all my cuts."

"He didn't even clean out the wound or give her shots for the pain," Pat says, bitterly. "He just stitched the jagged gashes and said, 'Never come back! If you do, I personally assure you will never leave alive!' So much for the Hippocratic Oath."

"Now you know why they call the Negro wing the butcher shop," Florence says. "One of you has to remove my stitches eventually. For now get the disinfectant and I'll scrub it as well as I can from the outside— and watch it like a hawk for any sign of infection."

In the silence that follows, someone notices Kenny's blackening eye. "What happened to you?" All faces turn to him and then to Lefty as they launch into our story. Kenny beaten. Lefty beaten to unconsciousness. Florence is precariously vulnerable. If a piece of glass had struck an artery, she'd be dead. An infection could still kill her. Singing "We Shall Overcome" might soothe my fear, but it won't erase the warning from the Negro youth in bib overalls echoing in my mind: you came here to die.

FIREBALL IN THE NIGHT

PINEVILLE
Friday, August 20

Past midnight two days later, our sheets thrown aside in the sultry air, Nellie, Carol and I fidget in the loft of the Freedom House. John, Herb and Henry try to sleep in the rooms behind the store. Fatigue, heat and a constant nagging fear drain our energy and our bodies crave sleep, but we are constantly on alert, listening for the crunch of tires on gravel in front of the store, the crash of shattering glass and the thump of a Molotov cocktail. Two months in Pineville have taken their emotional toll. For Herb and Henry, who live here, that toll continually assaults their being.

Night frightens us most because secrets happen in the dark. We can't escape in deep slumber, but occasionally there might be a tattered dream of home, the fleeting face of a boyfriend or the memory of sleeping in. Not tonight. A legion of mosquitoes plagues us, whining in the oppressive night and I feel as though the world is about to explode. I need to pee, but I don't dare walk down the outside stairs to the toilet. Something waits in the darkness. I know it as I drift off.

"Fire!"

It's a man's voice and I scramble to look out the window expecting the male workers' rooms to be engulfed in flames, but a dull red glow high-lights the horizon across the street accentuating silhouettes of loblolly and yellow pine.

"It's not here," I say. "Looks like it's over near Redeemer."

Pulling on our clothes we fly barefoot down the stairs. Mrs. Simmons waits next to her car. Her Negro face is fierce in Herb's headlights as he peels out of the parking lot with Carol and Henry. Nellie and I jump in the front seat of Mrs. Simmons's car and we follow the Pontiac toward the ominous glow. John stays behind, next to the phone.

"It looks like it might be Redeemer," I say.

Mrs. Simmons worships at Redeemer Reformed Episcopal Church and we've all attended weekly services there.

"Do you think it's the Klan?" I ask.

"You just be quiet now, you hear?" Mrs. Simmons says, both anger and resignation in her voice.

It's our fault. If we weren't here, there wouldn't be a fire. Then I look at Mrs. Simmons, her jaw set, her lips tight. Is she thinking the same thing?

We come around the bend and a blazing Redeemer fills our view.

"Lord, have mercy," Mrs. Simmons whispers. She steers the car onto the grassy shoulder and stops behind Herb.

"We are so sorry," Nellie breathes. And we are. Redeemer has been a base for our voter registration drive. Rev. Abraham Gadsden and many of the congregation supported the white civil rights workers in their midst at least once every week. When we take buses of folks to register to vote, we meet here. The church, surrounded by cotton fields on a rural road, obviously offered too tempting a target to those who would rid the community of outside agitators.

We leave the cars only to shrink from the blast of heat.

"Is that a fire truck?" Carol asks in disbelief as a truck passes us and pulls up to two houses on the right of the church. We all remember the empty truck when the elementary school burned.

"Thas Robert Bobbitt," Herb says. "The cotton gins his. He's a cracker, but he wants a local firehouse. The St. Stephen Fire Department is ten minutes away so he has his own truck."

Bobbitt begins running out hose and Herb and Henry hurry to help him. No hope for the church, but the houses might be saved.

"How'd it start?" Nellie asks.

Redeemer Reformed Episcopal Church the day after the fire

Mrs. Simmons the day after the fire

"Fire bomb," reports Herb. "White guys in a pickup truck."

A white pine tree explodes in a spray of sparks as the flames reach the branches, fence posts char and suddenly the second story of Redeemer collapses with a horrifying whoosh and thud. Mrs. Simmons shudders.

"Why did it burn so fast?" I ask. "It's brick."

"It's just veneer," she says simply. "We jus' finished it las' year. We pass that collection plate lots of Sundays to pay for that heap of rubble. Inside it was jus' an old frame church from 1911."

We stare, hypnotized for ten minutes as the flames die down and the fire is reduced to hot coals.

"The Lord works in mysterious ways His wonders to perform," Mrs. Simmons says as she turns away from the fire and strides back to the car as we hurry to follow. "Some folks is gon' be angry with me now, but most gon' be mad about our church. We need to plan a mass meetin'. The Lord's will be done."

She seems resigned, but I am far beyond the outrage I felt watching televised burning churches in Mississippi or Alabama. The Civil Rights Movement means Dr. Martin Luther King, Jr.; sit-ins; marches and Negroes voting for the first time. Outrage would be a relief from the guilt I now feel.

This is no longer an adventure or an opportunity to help others. Someone destroyed this House of God because we are here. Pineville is just a rural area, a wide spot on the road. Dr. Martin Luther King, Jr. didn't come here. It isn't part of a Supreme Court case changing the way people interact in the world. No news cameraman captures this devastation. We four came and the most obvious proof of our arrival lies blackened before us.

And tomorrow we canvass for voters, again.

ON THE OUTSIDE THINKING IN

PINEVILLE
Saturday, August 21

It's mid-August, the day after Redeemer burned and the search for beds for the guys has become constant. In June, John had three cluttered rooms downstairs behind the store to himself. Three dark, tiny rooms and four single beds. By August as many as twenty people vie for pillows and sheets. It's not unusual to find some fellow asleep in our meeting room.

The women were blessed with the best sleeping quarters when we arrived in June. We can easily accommodate six or more if necessary, and there's room on the floor for many more. Florence, Nellie and I now share the loft with Carol, who joined us from the Charleston project. Occasionally Julie, Joan or one of the other female volunteers comes up from Charleston for a day or two. John's sister Sally visited with us for awhile.

Truly, we never know who we will face over the breakfast grits or if that person will still be with us in the evening. Many days are dull, the same activities over and over: breakfast, canvass, write reports, hang out in the office, cook supper. On these days a new face is a pleasure—someone new to learn about. Other days are exciting—often too exciting, like the burning of the church—and then we welcome the safety in numbers.

Mrs. Simmons's meeting room, and when it rained, laundry-drying room

Our "family" changes under the direction of SCLC in Atlanta and the NAACP in Charleston. Staffers—always male—drop by from both to check our progress. For instance, SCLC sent Bob and Negro George. Lefty and Deke are from Charleston sent by the NAACP. Some of the younger, local Negro workers stay with us because their parents have thrown them out as long as they are involved in The Movement. Occasionally a friend from the training in Atlanta drops in. Meals might include visitors or local workers.

Although the population might change, there is one rule. No one leaves without telling Florence or John where they're going. If we're away from the Freedom House, we're expected to call in every hour, if possible. How else will they know we're safe?

We are under siege in our minds if not in fact. Reverend Middleton has stationed his nephew in the cornfield across the street. The nephew guards us with a shotgun. We rely on one another. We trust one another. We are like a large extended family with cousins coming and going.

And our family has pet names for one another. Nigger is not a word that I often heard in California. But I hear it all day now. "Hey Nigger," means hello to our Negro workers. Nigger is an exclamation, an appellation, a term of endearment. It is what members of the in-crowd call one another—if they are Negro.

Kenny Washington walks around the corner of the building this morning and approaches me. "Hey, Nigger," I welcome him. As the word slips from my lips he slaps me. My cheek smarts as I hear the smack and step back, breathing in a gulp. His brows knit together and he looks down at his hand quiet at his side. I wonder why he slapped me.

I won't cry, but tears press against my eyelids. The use of "nigger" was not addressed at orientation. Kenny and I sit in church together. We canvass together. We go to demonstrations together. We face the Klan together. I'm part of the in-crowd even if I am a white girl. Aren't I?

Is he as shocked that I'd call him nigger as I am that he'd slap me? I wonder as Kenny walks away.

There is a narrow line we walk as white people in a Negro world. We share ideas with the Negro workers, but we don't share history or skin color. We share church, canvassing, demonstrations and the Klan, but we don't feel the same way about these activities as our Negro friends do. I choose to believe there is family in his slap. We are close enough he can slap me like he might another Negro with no fear of retaliation based on color. It's a strange way of looking at the situation, but it's comforting.

Linda Darby

A LINE IN THE SAND: PROMISE

PINEVILLE
Wednesday, August 25

It's been five weeks since registration day when Mrs. Crawford failed to register and she has been steadily on my mind. Her courage and grit delight me, but canvassing through the community took longer than expected. The chaos of the last two weeks of direct action left little time for teaching someone to read. I need to be reminded of why I came south, so I finally tell Florence I have a promise to keep.

The road is just as long and as hot as before. Far ahead, I can see someone moving toward me. I recognize the straw hat first, then a basket on her arm and finally that beaming, delighted face.

"It's you!" She sets her basket down in the middle of the road and raises her arms to heaven as if in thanks. I shake her hand and smile back into her eyes.

Before I can say anything, she says, "Chile, Ah bin wonderin' where you was. Sunday Ah prayed that you come an' learn me how to write."

I explain I have been busy trying to get other folks to register.

"When Ah gots up this mornin' Ah was feeling something extra good was gon' happen today. Ah clean my house real good. Ah felt so gran' Ah come on down the road. Ah saw you an' Ah knew what that good was. Look what Ah can do."

She bends down and picks up a stick. With a steady hand she writes **Rebecca** slowly and deliberately in the sand.

Rebecca

RIDING THE WAVE

PINEVILLE
Wednesday, August 25

"BLACK MEN DON'T LET SUNDOWN CATCH YOU IN ST. STEPHEN," warn the letters scrawled across a piece of cardboard in red paint. Someone discovered it nailed to a fence post near the Freedom House yesterday. Owned and run by white people, St. Stephen is the closest commercial area to Pineville. It's the, "You to Blondie," [sic] scribbled next to "sundown" that gets my attention. What did I do to earn a personal threat? Enough is enough and I'm ready to go home—home to California.

Now it's close to midnight and I'm on guard in front of Mrs. Simmons's house, but I'm not alone. The "sign" has us even edgier; being "on guard" has an urgency it didn't have earlier in the summer. Charley (a white worker from Charleston) and I guard the front of the Freedom House from behind one of the cars. Charley carries a shotgun.

"White Ford pickup, number 6, Charlie, 9, 7, 2, Bravo, November," he calls to me farther back from the road. I write down the license plate and wait.

Carol and Walter (a new Negro volunteer) are across the street sitting

Kenny Washington and Bobby Gadsden with Ku Klux Klan sign found nailed to a fence post near the Freedom House

on the ground behind a car at the Snipe home. Occasionally I can hear them murmuring.

Herb protects the landing upstairs with a shotgun. Lefty covers the branch (creek) behind the store with a handgun. Some of us may be nonviolent, but not all of us. For those who aren't, self-defense is more important than philosophy.

Our direct action has angered enough people that the sign painter and others want to block Negro access to the stores in town. The sign provokes a Pineville community meeting to which we aren't invited. At the meeting the Negro settlement declares a boycott of St. Stephen until certain demands are met: a Negro policeman, Negroes on the Trustee Board, Negro boys and girls hired in the stores and no more police brutality and injustice. Abolishing the Ku Klux Klan is the final issue.

When we leave, the boycott will still be in place, those involved enticing others to join.

The last two weeks have been like riding a tidal wave. Waves of violence and a search for justice vie with swells of anticipation, dread and emotional exhaustion. The Berkeley Restaurant, Howard's Restaurant and the burning of Redeemer Reformed Episcopal Church were the "big" events, but there were smaller ones as well.

When we drove into the parking lot from watching the Redeemer fire, John yelled from the top of the store, "Take cover! Take cover!" A pickup had driven by and the occupants fired six .22 shots and one shotgun blast into the store.

On the same day, Reverend Willie Middleton, who carried workers to canvass in his old car, was arrested for having the wrong signal indicator on.

"Boy," white men threatened the Reverend, "You stay away from them white folks or we'll keep you away." At seventy-two he's a tough old bird who ignores the threat.

About one o'clock the next morning someone threw gasoline bombs inside the Swamp Fox, a white mini-appliance place and the only store in the area with a Negro working on the counter. The front windows were

Reverend Willie Middleton

blasted out and the shelves, merchandise and televisions disappeared in flames.

The evening after the Berkeley Restaurant and Howard's Restaurant incidents Kenny Washington went to court in St. Stephen. He had been arrested for driving fifty in a thirty-five mile zone, although he was actually doing thirty. His trial brought out thirty Negroes from Pineville, much to our surprise. Their purpose: to see to it he gets a fair trial.

We waited for the judge for over an hour, packed into a room about the size of a living room. When the judge finally arrived, he ordered, "Get all these people out of here. This ain't goin' be no show. Everybody out but the witnesses, lawyers and defendant!"

Downstairs we faced about forty angry white men and the police chief who insisted, "Y'all have to vacate the premises. No loitering here."

Moments later, on the way out of town, John and his passenger were driven off the road and John took several blows from the men in that car before he got his car started and drove away.

Sandwiched somewhere between threats there were days we stagnated, now that we were no longer canvassing. I wrote in my journal, "Things are pretty bad here. This last week the weather has been hotter than usual. We're under the pressure of waiting for something we have no idea about. We're tired. Staff relations are slipping. We snap at one another and slights we would have forgiven easily fester. I almost wish something would happen so we'd have excitement for awhile—a period of letting go usually follows."

The day I wrote this we got comic relief of a sort. We were visited by two law enforcement agencies.

The FBI came in the morning. Two gentlemen in suits came by to "investigate the events that have gone on in St. Stephen and Moncks Corner."

"We are particularly interested in gathering evidence in the school fire," one of them said. We know the FBI won't follow up on any evidence they find. In civil rights circles they are notorious for watching civil rights workers beaten and churches burned. They collect evidence, but never do anything to help.

In the afternoon, we are visited by SLED (South Carolina Law Enforcement Division). This was where the comedy comes in.

"We know there's been trouble here," one of them began. "We're here to find out what you did to cause someone to burn down a church and set fire to a school." They considered us outside agitators. If we would just go home.

On August 23, Reverend Middleton was arrested again. This time for assault and carrying dangerous weapons. His bail, $165, used the last of our budget. He swore he stopped to drop some people off to catch a bus and the next thing he knew, a cop was searching his car. Of course, he carries a shotgun and a knife in the trunk.

The same night a Negro was beaten attempting to shop at Powell's Red and White Market, owned by whites.

I shift my weight to stand on the other foot and realize it's asleep. I catch myself before I fall, shake my foot to consciousness and stare into the darkness listening to crickets and mosquitoes.

Later tonight I will write in my journal, "I want to be a typical teenager. I want to go home." But, before I finally fall asleep I realize I can never be a "typical" teenager again. Standing guard against the Klan is not something most teenagers do.

Demonstration in Charleston supporting the Voting Rights Act of 1965: Doris Rose is second in line and then Sherie Holbrook.

WE DON'T SERVE COLORED
PEOPLE HERE: POLITICS

MONCKS CORNER
Thursday, August 26

Eight days after we were locked out, we're back at Howard's Restaurant and this time we get in. A red-faced Mr. Howard slaps each of the menus down, one by one. The glasses of water hit the tablecloth with a smack. He glares at the sheriff stationed at the door, turns and storms into the kitchen, infuriated that he must serve us.

What we order is not important. We are here to be served that order. The sheriff fidgets and looks at the floor as he unwillingly enforces the 1964 Civil Rights Act. Outside the door, two burly sheriffs scan the street and wait. We have a right to be here, but the six of us are poised and uneasy in our chairs. We are the only patrons. How did we get in this time?

Seven days ago, the day after we were attacked outside Moncks Corner, Florence called the sheriff collect as he'd requested. She explained his responsibility according to the federal law. She pointed out that people had been injured by local bullies.

"We were disappointed," she said into the phone, "to find that you were powerless to keep us safe as you promised." We all listened, smiles on our faces. She was discouraged yesterday, but her determined attitude is back today.

"We have no alternative but to file lawsuits against the Berkeley Restaurant and Howard's Restaurant. Our intention is to contact the Southern Christian Leadership Conference and request that they send buses of workers to Moncks Corner. There are other businesses we can visit. Perhaps the news media would like to cover such an event." We could hear the sheriff's voice squawking on the other end, but we didn't know what he was saying. Eventually Florence said that "we can agree to that."

The first real smile of the summer spread across her face as she put the phone down and looked up at us.

(l to r) Louis Bryant, Julie TenBrink and Ike Williams

"It seems," she said, "that the sheriff is very sorry we were attacked. He would like to offer us an alternative to the actions I described to him."

"We could file a lawsuit," Carol said.

"But we'll never get buses of workers from SCLC," John said. "So, what's his alternative?"

"Lunch at Howard's." She looked so satisfied.

Anticlimax. That's what we feel. So much happened just to order the hamburgers that arrive from the kitchen. There's no fanfare. No celebration. Everyone is uncomfortable: the police, Mr. Howard, his waitresses and us. However, no one misses the point that those burgers have been served to Negroes and to people who want to eat with Negroes. I hardly taste each bite I'm so overcome with what we have accomplished. Lefty will say later that the burgers slaked our hunger and satisfied our souls. They did more than that. They provided the proof that we had won!

BETWEEN TWO WORLDS

⌐

That night, after our triumphant burgers in Moncks Corner we have our last group meeting, our opportunity to "tell it like it was" and trace our progress individually and as a team.

"It seems like years ago now, but remember tha' night a pickup full of Klansmen followed us, so we cut off the lights an' took a dirt road off the highway?" Willie Louis Prioleau, Ishmael Prioleau's younger brother and a volunteer worker, refers to an evening in June when we were returning from a mass meeting. "It was like a movie when we lost 'em."

"Ah remember prayin' that pickup wouldn't follow us," Kenny replies. "And Ah don' pray at movies."

"The night we went to the Star Theater was worse," Ishmael says. "We walked out that theater that night an' there was a bunch of angry white folks. Man, they had sticks an' bottles an' rocks. Remember those white guys came after us an' shot at us? They did some shootin', now." Our relationship has been project-oriented since John's threat, but his voice brings me an old longing.

We reminisce about some of the terrifying incidents we shared. Then the conversation turns to preparing for demonstrations. In Atlanta, we'd learned about nonviolence, but they didn't tell us that most of the people in the communities we entered might not be nonviolent at all. Nor did

George Simmons
in front of the
SCOPE office

they explain how we would get them to give up their weapons for direct action.

"One of the biggest surprises we got when we came here," Nellie says, "was that almost all of you carried weapons—knives and even guns. I was so amazed when Reverend Middleton came into the office to tell us that his nephew had a shotgun in the cornfield cross the way."

"That meant so much," I say. "When I thanked his nephew last week he said, 'We takes care of our own.' I felt like I belonged."

Maxine nods, "Remember the day you an' Mae an' me went to St. Stephen? We never got such mean stares in our lives befo'."

"Oh, and that guy called me a blond nigger," I pretend to preen in front of a mirror.

"That was my first time bein' followed by a car full of white men," Mae says. "Funny how Ah got used to it."

We sip our Nehis and look at one another. This will be the last time we are all together. We started as strangers of different races, now we feel like family.

"Girl, you was always talkin' 'bout integratin' the schools an' you says Negro schools ain't as good as white," Kenny challenges, as if he really was my brother. "But you ain't bin to a Negro school. You wants us to take the chance, but you won't do youself."

"You're right," I say. "Tell you what. You get me an application to a Negro college and I'll fill it out. If they accept me, I'll go." I feel cocky. I know he'll never find one here.

"Ah'll have that paper tomorrow," he says. I think he's all talk, but in the morning he hands me an application to Allen University in Columbia, South Carolina. As he watches, I fill it out and send it off. (I'm back in California when I hear I've been accepted to attend and I will spend the first semester of my sophomore year there as the only white student.)

"Henry, are you still not speaking to your father?" I ask, turning from Kenny. Henry has seemed mute most of the summer. He moved in with us after his father kicked him out of the house for working with us. Although he talked a little with some of us, he still had to summon courage to talk to most white folks.

"Yeah. We talkin'," he says. "When y'all leave, Ah'll go home."

Nellie said, "Kenny's grandfather said just yesterday that he can't work with us anymore. He doesn't want white men sneaking around the house."

"None of us do!" Henry almost smiled.

"Seriously, though," Nellie says. "Look at all we did in less than nine weeks. Over three hundred and fifty people were registered to vote in the two days the books were open and more will be next month."

Was it only nine weeks? I think. I've known these people and this place all my life, haven't I? I don't remember who I was before Pineville, South Carolina. What will I do about that when I go home?

"We finally ate at Howard's," I add, remembering the others, "even though some places closed rather then integrate." Other restaurants became private clubs to keep us from trying to get in.

"Remember our first meetin'?" Butch comments, stretching out his legs. "When we came to that meetin' we had no idea what to expect. We sure wondered what four white people was doin' in Pineville."

"That meeting is not one of my favorite memories," I say. "I felt like a fool talking to an audience of deaf people. Y'all just sat there."

"We didn't know how to act. We never seen any white people who wanted to treat us equally," Butch says.

"We had no idea how to act, either," Nellie says. "We had training but sometimes it seemed pretty useless. We knew the youth group had to be powerful for the summer's success. We expected you to be more excited about The Movement coming to your community."

"Oh, Ah always get excited thinkin' 'bout gettin' shot or havin' my house burnt down," Mae says ruefully.

"You have a point," I respond. "Did any of you forget yourselves this summer?"

"Girl, whatcha' talkin' about, forget ourselves?" Maxine demands.

"We were here about four weeks the first time I forgot color," I say. "It's not that I forgot you are Negroes, it's that I forgot I was white. We were at a meeting and I suddenly felt we were just people together. I wasn't a stranger. I was just part of a community."

"Anytime you want to remember about color," Willie Louis says, "all you has to do is walk through St. Stephen with one of us. The stares an' nasty comments will remind you."

We smile at one another and I realize no one continuously fends off the heat with his/her fan. It's still hot but more bearable, offering perhaps, the faint hope of fall.

"We're leaving tomorrow," Nellie says. "How do y'all feel about this summer?"

"Theys bin real change," Ishmael says. "The kind of change that's forever." He winks at me and I'm sure I blush.

"That's the truth," Butch adds. "Our lives were conditioned to accept things as they were, because change had never bin a part of our lives."

"Then you four comes, an' we sees lots of possibilities we didn't think about," says Kenny. "Civil rights stuff was for folks in Mississippi an' Alabama."

"You brought it here to us an' nothin's the same now," Mae says. "Martin Luther King came to us through y'all."

I'm moved beyond comment.

Unsure that we spoke a common language, we struggled to talk to one another at our first meeting in July. It is the same tonight, even though we now share a language molded by events and emotions the summer brought us. Unsure how to say good-bye to the passion and trust we've shared, we end the meeting in our usual "see you tomorrow" mode. I feel confident this is not our "end." After all, I have everyone's address. They are only a stamp away.

Mrs. Simmons's Head Start School, November 1965

Although I miss my family, I don't want to leave Pineville. The friends I've made and the satisfaction I've gotten from involvement in the community embrace me.

In fourteen hours, I travel ahead to the twentieth century, arriving in New York City. I stay with the family of Shelly, another civil rights worker I'd met in Atlanta. Amazingly, my transition back to "real" life takes several years to accomplish. I find myself afraid of white people and the police regardless of their race. I had lost my sense of color only to regain it with a rush—an unsettling problem.

While visiting with my family in California, I feel utterly adrift and lost. I call Pineville and speak with Lefty who informs me that I've been accepted by Allen University, an all-Negro college in Columbia, South Carolina. The NAACP in Columbia will support me as long as I attend Allen.

My father threatens never to speak to me if I go, but my mother drives me to the airport. (My father's threat only lasts until I call home the first time.) While I'm not excluded at Allen, I'm a conspicuous stranger from another world and the students are friendly enough, but cautious. For me, the strain of being constantly "on stage" is wearing and leaves me lonely. I intend to stay at Allen at least a year, but loneliness and the realization that Allen cannot offer the education the University of California does, shortens my stay to one semester. When I started at Berkeley, I was just another blond in cut-offs and a tee shirt trying to get to class. At Allen I'm a symbol of the future. My experience as the only white student on a historically black campus and the quality of that education are topics for another book.

When I return to the University of California in the fall of 1966, I move into the black ghetto in Berkeley where I feel comfortable. I attend classes at the university, but my residence and social life are where I feel safe—with Negro families.

LOOKING BACK

"**Dreams are illusions . . .
from the book your soul is writing about you.**"
Marsha Norman, 1983 Pulitzer Prize winner
for her play *'Night Mother*

Did I expect that something I did would change the world? I hoped so, though our project was like a pebble dropped into an immense pool. There were no waves like Dr. King's "I Have a Dream" speech or the Selma-to-Montgomery March or a Supreme Court decision to mark our presence in Pineville. Forty plus years later, the Pineville area still seems exclusively black. Our project simply started ripples of understanding which had not been present before.

I think the most important thing I did was to be there. Just as Shirley shared her pennies with me that morning in church, I shared my thoughts and emotions, my physical being and my commitment. I was white and they were black, but we were all human and we only needed to learn about one another to know that. We didn't always see the world the same way, but we saw it together and were willing to try to understand the myriad ways of noticing.

Our gains were small individually, but together became part of the rising tide of change. Although John, Kenny and Lefty were assaulted and Florence hurled through a glass door, no one suffered lasting injury.

Redeemer Reformed Episcopal Church was rebuilt. In 2008, the *Columbia Star* (Columbia, South Carolina) writer Warner M. Montgomery wrote: "A week after the fire . . . the Bishop, pastor, and men of the church each pledged $100 and the women pledged fifty dollars. In ninety days, there was enough to proceed (to build a new church). After four years worshipping in a tent or at a school, the new church welcomed its congregation in 1969."

When the Klan sign warned the Negro community to stay out of St. Stephen, the community began a boycott. I was there when it began, but I'm not sure when it ended. I know it was still in place in October of that year, but by the time I visited at Christmas, it was over. St. Stephen had hired George Simmons to be the first black policeman.

What did we leave undone? The project lasted a few months after we left with Herb, Butch, Lefty and Marion (a new black worker from Charleston) hanging on as long as they could. They registered 210 voters in September. Herb was the last member to leave and he registered twenty by himself in October. That made our total registered 580. We worked only nine weeks and started from scratch, so we celebrated our accomplishment. The money raised in Berkeley, California, to support our project was exhausted on the purchase of a car, car care and gasoline, bail, office supplies, Mae and Maxine's pay, and telephone service, among other operating costs. SCLC could not finance an ongoing project in the Pineville area.

None of our local workers attended an integrated high school. In an e-mail in 2008, Earl Williams, a local retired high school administrator, explains when integration occurred this way, "First desegregation of the schools in Berkeley County officially began in the fall of 1971. (I recall because I was one of the many teachers transferred to achieve racial equality.) The focus seemed to have been on an exchange of black teachers from predominantly black schools with teachers from predominantly white schools. In the first few years there were no significant differences in the number of students of both races entering different schools. Many of the white parents chose to enroll their kids in private schools and here in St. Stephen they even created a private school for their students to attend rather than allow them to attend school with black students."

334 Auburn Ave., N.E.
Atlanta, Georgia 30303
Telephone 522-1420

Southern Christian Leadership Conference

Martin Luther King Jr., *President*   Ralph Abernathy, *Treasurer*   Andrew J. Young, *Executive Director*

October 1, 1965

Dear SCOPE Volunteer,

It is a rare privilege in life to participate in the fulfillment of an idea whose time has come. Your involvement with the SCOPE Project this summer was such a privilege. For, whether you realize it or not, you were a part of a history-making enterprise which has gripped us all in its infinite garment of destiny. We of the Southern Christian Leadership Conference were indeed fortunate to have had you as one of our volunteers. We will be forever grateful to you for the sacrifices which you made in coming down and for the dedication and devotion to the cause of human rights and dignity which you shared with so many of "the least of these, my brethren", in the course of the summer.

It will be some time before we can adequately assess the results of this summer. The delay in passage of the Voting Rights Bill meant that the actual addition of voters was not what it might have been, but you broke much new ground and laid a solid foundation upon which we will continue to build for years to come. This foundation may soon become the cornerstone of our democracy, for the unregistered Negro voters in the South may well determine whether our Congress is one which progressively and creatively faces the future or whether it becomes like some of the do-nothing Congresses of the past. Our world demands the very best that this country can give if the elements of people around the world are to share in the abundant life.

I have enclosed a brief questionnaire in which I would appreciate your very frank and candid evaluation of your work this summer. We entered this project under great strain and following directly on the heels of the Selma campaign, so we know that we made many mistakes. However, we must be aware of these mistakes that they might be corrected in future efforts and that we might continue to grow to meet the challenge which is upon us.

Again, let me extend my warmest and most heartfelt congratulations for a job well done.

Sincerely yours,

Martin Luther King, Jr.

MLK, Jr. :df
Enclosures

By the time I graduated from Berkeley in 1968 I knew I had to be a teacher. Where else could I inspire tolerance, responsibility and freedom? I intended to teach in inner-city schools, but my first position was near my parents in an all-white world. I later moved to suburban Sacramento schools where I taught thirty-one years in continuation schools for at-risk students.

Did I make a difference? I know I did. I've kept in touch with many of the people who befriended me that summer and those relationships led to this book and hopefully to another. The young man in bib overalls in Atlanta was right. Part of me did die in 1965. But a struggling new self emerged and it's a strong attribute of who I am today. I'm still not all I want to be, but I'm working on it.

EPILOGUE

It was 2005 when I opened my forty-year-old journal to find hazy memories there. Some events were vibrant and those events involved the few folks I'd kept in touch with through letters, phone calls and occasional visits. So I interviewed volunteers and people from Pineville to refresh my memories of events and study the impact of our project.

A shift in culture was the most obvious in my 2006 interview with Ishmael Prioleau, then fifty-eight, divorced and a father of four. In 1965, I couldn't "see" him because a mixed couple might spoil the impact of the project and endanger us. Forty years later my husband videotapes our interview. The volunteers and supporters of the Pineville SCOPE project had given it heart and vigor. Between us, Ishmael and I could account for several of our fellow workers. What do they remember and where are they now?

Sitting comfortably at a kitchen table in Pineville, we laugh at how I'd almost been sent home and how afraid we had been of being caught together. My husband laughs with us as he patiently runs the camera.

Ishmael's first disclosure is a total surprise to me. He's looking through the pictures I'd brought to jumpstart memories. "When they broke the glass here (pointing at a picture of the school office), Ah saw when they did that. Three or four white men at the time and they broke the glass and

Ah saw them throw somethin' inside. They wanted to burn the records and so forth, because they didn't want integration to come about."

"How do you know that?" I'm astonished.

"My bedroom window in my father's house overlooked the school."

"You saw who did it and you never told—not even us?"

"My dad was afraid because we lived right on the road." He continued, "And, so when the FBI and those came, Ah started to tell them what Ah saw, but he [my father] told me not to say anythin'. He was afraid because in the past they had burned people out. They would come by and shoot and you don't know who would get shot or killed. That's the reason why he never allowed me to tell."

"J. K. school was set on fire and Redeemer was burned to the ground," I say. "Do you think what we did was worth it?"

"Some things, some bad things, happened, but a lot of times to get some things to come to the forefront, some bad things have to happen. Even though the church burned down, it was replaced with a better building. And then sometimes a thing will just happen and also bring people closer together; because they really see there is a need for them to get together, work together and strive to make things better. We had more of a sense of togetherness at that time, Ah think. We'd gotten to the point that we knew some things had to happen for change to come about. Once folks got that votin' fever, they [white folks] had to give a listenin' ear to some of our demands to bring about changes."

"You were a senior after the summer of '65," I say. "What did you do after high school?"

"Ah went to Morris College and got a teaching credential. Ah came home to teach here. Ah got married and had four children. Now Ah'm retired, but Ah tutor some."

"And I substitute some," I tell him. "Several of us went into teaching."

"My brother Willie Louis did. He became a teacher, married Treasure, raised a family and retired. He lives over in the Peru section. You know, the only three jobs for an 'educated Negro' then were teachin', preachin' or undertakin'."

"Julie TenBrink is a retired teacher. She still lives in Modesto. She has a daughter. When I interviewed her she was still teaching, though. She said, 'I tell my students about Martin Luther King, and show signs (enforcing segregation) from the '50s to share that story and time. I'm still a warrior in the classroom in that way, to still fight for those principles of fairness and equality.'"

"I remember Julie, but I really remember Nellie. What happened to her?"

"In 1965, Nellie Habegger was already married when we came from California. She left her husband at home working on his Ph.D."

"He let her come down here?"

"You know about independent women. What could he do? She'd made up her mind." We both chuckle.

"What does she think looking back?"

"I think Nellie was the most dissatisfied of the folks I've interviewed. When I first wrote to her, she wrote back, '"I've always felt our mission in Pineville was something of a failure. We went there primarily to do voter registration, but when we got to our destination it seems we became distracted or at least didn't know how to energize our project. We visited churches and spoke of the importance of the vote, but I remember doing very little actual voter registration or teaching others the process.'"

"Did she remember we could only actually register voters one day a month?"

"She remembered, but the burning of Redeemer was so shocking to us, I don't think those of us from the West Coast ever really recovered from the responsibility," I admit. "Nellie felt that 'we landed in Pineville, created a big ruckus, and then scooted out of town at summer's end. Soon after Redeemer burned we were gone forever, leaving y'all behind in the summer's rubble pile.'"

"Y'all?"

"Hey, I remember some of what I learned. Y'all is perfect for a classroom of kids."

"You mentioned Carol."

"Carol Sanders went back to California and graduated from the University of California with a degree in criminology. Where Nellie felt the project lacked vigor, Carol found her own discrimination when she came home. This time she was the target. Police departments wouldn't hire women. She went back to school to become a nurse. She married, had two sons, divorced and remarried. She lives in the Bay Area of California. I'm wondering about Butch Summers. His dad abused him to keep him from working for us, but it didn't help. He was from Pineville, but he's gone now. What have you heard from him?"

"I remember he says I borrowed a book I haven't returned. I didn't borrow it."

"That's not exactly what I meant."

Ishmael grinned, "Butch graduated from South Carolina State College after a tour of duty in Vietnam. You know he thought school desegregation was hardest on the black community. Black teachers were fired first. More importantly, white parents would not allow black teachers to discipline their children, so more private schools were built to accommodate whites. Butch and his wife, Mozetta, moved to North Carolina to get a better education for their two boys. His oldest graduated from high school and is in prep school for the Air Force Academy."

"Where is Mae Simmons?"

"She lives in New York with her husband, who isn't very well. She has two daughters. One is an attorney and the other is an insurance claims representative. I asked her if she'd do civil rights work again. She answered, 'If need be, I'd do it again.'"

"Does Linda Darby still live nearby? I know she didn't get to work with us as much as she wanted to because her mother was ill."

"She lives in St. Stephen. Both of her children went to college in the North. Her daughter went to school in Oregon and her son in Vermont. She also raised a niece who became a nurse. The last time I talked to her she said, 'I sent them [my kids] places where they had to interact with whites.'"

Neither of us spoke for a moment. We both knew Maxine Ravenell, who along with Lula Mae Simmons was one of our paid workers, had married, had three children and passed away at thirty-six with breast cancer.

"So, who is this Herb Mitchell I've been hearing about?" Joe asked, bringing us both back to the present.

"We could go down to the Huddle House to see Herb. He doesn't work there, but he does hang out there," Ishmael says. "After our summer project he went to Alabama to register voters."

"He worked in Alabama, too?" I asked.

"Remember when he, Lefty and Butch went to Georgia for more training? Well, Herb made connections then. When our project wound down, he went to Alabama."

"What does he talk about when looking back?" I ask.

"Folks change. He said that he wouldn't want his kids doing what we did because it was too dangerous. He even said he wouldn't do it now. That's probably because he's over sixty." He grinned again.

"How many children did he have?"

"He had four and they all graduated from college."

"Ishmael, do you remember Ray Nelson? He worked mostly in Charleston, but he came out this way from time to time."

"He had a VW bug?"

"Oh, he sure did. I rode all the way from California to Charleston in that bug."

"He did some work with us out near Hugar."

"That's him. He's sixty-four. You and I used to talk about how you didn't want to be a preacher. Well, he became one. He's married and lives in Texas with his wife who is also a minister."

"Yaas, the Lord never called me." And this time Ishmael really smiles.

"I took Joe to see the Freedom House." I look over at Joe. "What a disappointment. The house, the office with the loft and the Simmons house are all buried in jungle. We managed to fight our way in, but it was a bit like visiting a cemetery—nothing alive but the woods."

"Bin growing that way since Mrs. Simmons went to live with her kids in New York and New Jersey in '85 or '86."

"Mrs. Simmons wrote to me when her husband, George, died. She sent me one of the programs from his funeral."

"Now there was a fellow with a sense of humor," Ishmael says. "After the boycott of St. Stephen he was chosen to be the first black police officer around here."

"I talked to Mrs. Simmons about a year before she died. She didn't remember me, but she did remember that summer."

"The Legislature of the State of South Carolina even passed a resolution on her behalf after she passed."

"She certainly made history happen in Pineville."

Rte. 1, Box 24
Pineville, S.C. 29468

Dear Sherrie:

The Message of Sympathy from you brought Joy to my Heart. To know someone cares. George went home to live with the Lord in about, 10 minutes, He was getting ready to go to work 7:00 and pass 6:00 a.m.

I would like for you to make any Charity, give to these , poor Children, at the Berkeley County Citizen Day Care, Story Books, or Pictures, any kind of Teaching Material for ages: 3&4.

You must pray for us and we will pray for you, Hopeing to come to California soon, for a minute of rest.

Very Truly Yours

Martha P. Simmons

Martha P. Simmons

This is a letter from Mrs. Simmons on the death of her husband, George. Notice she is looking for materials for her day care center.

ACKNOWLEDGMENTS

To say that *I* wrote this book would be like Deke saying he made the hogshead stew. Without Deke's efforts, we would not have had a fine dinner and without my experiences we would not have this book. Deke butchered the hog, borrowed the ingredients and put them all together to simmer, but an elderly gentleman had raised the hog and given it as a gift. Someone grew and picked the corn. Someone else offered the beans. Okra came from another garden, as did the field peas. Each ingredient had been nurtured and we celebrated the combination of all of them.

And so it is with "my" book. The book idea came from Eleanor Wolf, as did hours of consultation, and more hours of editing, a satisfying friendship and great lunches. Her husband, Woody Rupp, edited reams and insisted I join Toastmasters to learn how to tell my stories. Sonja Bertolucci edited at the beginning and fielded questions about bibliographies and footnotes toward the end. All three got frantic phone calls and e-mails when I got stuck.

Marilyn (Lynn) Pribus is my good-natured, patient and perceptive editor. Her probing questions made me search for how I really felt and acted—after all, I was looking back forty years. How can I thank someone who helped me find myself; there were times when she seemed to know me better than I did.

Acknowledgments

Many of Lynn's factual questions were answered by Earl Williams, who lives in Pineville today. Researching the name of a laundry soap product or the cost of a Pontiac in South Carolina in the 1960s—specifically in one community—is where he excelled. If I needed to know someone or something local, it was Earl I e-mailed.

I thank the volunteers who shared their time and memories with me: Nellie Habegger; Carol Sanders Hanig; Herb Mitchell; Ray Nelson; Ishmael Prioleau, Jr.; James Summers; Lula Mae Simmons; Linda Darby; and Julie TenBrink.

Our project existed in a community and I learned about context from people who lived/had lived in Pineville: Ryan Alston, Brianna Blair, Albertha Butler, Emma Butler, Henry Butler, Leroy Butler, Fortrena Haskell, Joseph H. Jefferson, Coretta Simmons, Albert Smalls, Chequetta Smalls, Gwen Smalls, Henry Smalls, Gregory Sumpter, Lavonda Smalls, Lottie Smalls (my sister-by-choice), Ontario Smalls, Theresa Sumpter, De Vante Theirse, Shakara Theirse, Lucille Washington, Deborah Williams, Linda Darby Wilson and again, Earl Williams.

Alex Moore, acquisitions editor at the University of South Carolina, delighted me when he told me that, "We've never seen anything like this before—and that's a very good thing." He convinced me that the book had substance and real value.

Bud Gardner, writing coach extraordinaire, got me to write and submit a story to *Chicken Soup for the African American Woman's Soul.* That story, "A Line in the Sand," is the acorn from which the tree grew into *You Came Here to Die, Didn't You.* He introduced me to Lynn Pribus and wrote a blurb for this book.

The *Chicken Soup for the African American Women's Soul* staff and contributors not only published my story, they taught me about the advertising side of the book-selling process, including book signings, book tours and my first conference call.

Bettina Flores, author of *Chiquita's Cocoon*, was my cheerleader.

The pictures in this book are old and most are copies. I had to get high-resolution copies made of them. Chris Baird at Kinko's in Roseville, California, was my consultant for things photographic.

When I decided I needed a webpage, my nephew, Rocco Palladino filled that need. Lisa Lashley is my webmaster now.

Have you ever gotten stuck and been unable to find the answer? Me, too, so many times. Thank you to Paula Scardamalia who solved one of the organizational problems, suggested Mary Jo Zazueta guide me through the self-publishing process, and gave me an idea for the next book.

Thank you to Mary Jo. I was almost banging my head against the wall when I contacted her. She was patient when I wouldn't decide on a cover format and convinced me I'd made the right decision when I finally did.

Although our wedding vows included "for richer or poorer, in sickness and in health," they did not mention "when writing a book." My husband is my editor on demand. The Super Bowl, the World Series, the Master's Tournament, the Kentucky Derby, a good book—he let me interrupt them all to check my grammar and to comment on my ideas. And there were all those days I locked myself in the den. Thank you for your patience and sense of humor, Joe.

Two weeks before she passed away in 2004, I explained to my mother that as I'd grown older I could imagine how terrified she and my father must have been when I left for Atlanta in 1965. Her response was an echo of something I'd said long ago, "Somebody had to do it." Thank you, Mom.

Over five years a community grew around the idea of *You Came Here to Die, Didn't You,* just as a stew simmered with Deke's assistance. Without that community, there would be no book. Thank you, all.

APPENDIX A

Pineville Freedom House Staff
and Local Workers

———

Here is a list of people who worked on the Pineville project. If there is no comment behind a name, I was unable to locate that person.

White Volunteers from California in Charleston and Pineville

University of California, Berkeley
    Florence Jones – deceased
    John Kimball – deceased
    Sherie Holbrook Labedis – retired teacher and writing
      in California
    Pat Lang
    Ray Nelson – now a minister in Texas
    Carol Sanders – retired and living in California

Stanford University, Palo Alto
    Nellie Habegger – living in Oregon

Modesto Junior College
    Julie TenBrink – retired teacher living in California

Sonoma Community College
    Joan Kennedy

Black Volunteers from Berkeley County – Teenagers

Abraham

Alfonso

Azell Gilliard

Linda Ann Darby – retired teacher, now a Head Start center supervisor, living in St. Stephen, South Carolina

Bobby Gadsden – living in Philadelphia, Pennsylvania

Laurence

Beatrice Lloyd

Henry Moultrie

Ishmael Prioleau, Jr. – retired teacher living in Pineville, South Carolina

Willie Louis Prioleau – retired teacher living in Pineville, South Carolina

Maxine Ravenell – deceased

Roger Ravenell – living in Pineville, South Carolina

Doris Rose – deceased

Lulu Mae Simmons – living in Elmont, New York

James "Butch" Summers – retired and living in North Carolina

Joe Swinton

Vaughn

Walter

Kenny Washington

Black Volunteers from Berkeley County – Adults

Reverend Willie Middleton – deceased

Herb Mitchell – retired and living in St. Stephen

George Simmons – deceased

Martha Prioleau Simmons – deceased

Black Staff Workers from Charleston

Louis (Lefty) Bryant

Deke (Leon) White

APPENDIX B

People

I did not only interview volunteers. I also interviewed people from the community who were not involved in The Movement particularly, but who can speak to what living in Pineville was like before, during and after 1965. I've also interviewed the children of volunteers to see how their expectations differed from their folks.

HENRY BUTLER

Henry Butler, 67, did not live in Pineville in 1965, but he was raised there. When we talked he made the following point about the teenagers we worked with.

"You cannot imagine the total fear those children felt when they went with you to do the things you all did. Rest assured those were very fearful times for black people and we had to pretend. I can just imagine seeing them pretending; pretending everything was okay. . . . You saw lots of acting. They had to. They had to pretend that they didn't know, but they knew exactly what was going on."

JOSEPH H. JEFFERSON

Representative Joseph Jefferson, fifty-eight in 2006, speaks for Berkeley County in the South Carolina House of Representatives. Although he was not involved in our project, he took advantage of the changes and went into politics.

"I remember when you all were here. I was a senior. My parents said, 'Stay away. Don't get involved. There will be bloodshed.'

"When I went to college I was on the frontlines of the Orangeburg Massacre.[1]

"A Reverend Thomas Myers, who taught history, was really inspired during the time you all were here because prior to that all the voting precinct managers, vice presidents, presidents and other executive officers were all white. We didn't have blacks in the precincts. It's because the officers would go in early and somebody would make a motion, 'I move that we retain existing officers.' They just carried it, and boom, that was the end of it. If you weren't on time or before time, you wouldn't accomplish anything.

"Around '68 or '69 we were there about five minutes ahead of schedule. When they opened everything up, and when the same person made the same motion, we were there. That's when we started getting blacks involved in office holding."

Joe then related this story to me. It describes living a pattern that was not unusual in Pineville.

"My father was a principal and my mother was a school teacher, so we were sheltered. Anything derogatory or demeaning they'd made sure that we weren't part of.

"I didn't realize how black I was basically until I left home. When I was a little boy and we were traveling I thought it was a normal thing to not be able to get out of your car to go to a restaurant and to use its

---

1. "Three students were killed during a violent confrontation with law enforcement officials on the campus of South Carolina State University, February 8, 1968."

"The massacre was the culmination of three nights of escalating racial tension caused by the students' efforts to desegregate the All Star Bowling Lanes. S.C. highway patrolmen fired on a crowd, killing Samuel Hammond Jr., Delano Middleton and Henry Smith, and wounding 27 others. This tragedy was the first of its kind on any American college campus." The Official Tourism Site of the State of South Carolina. South Carolina Department of Parks, Recreation & Tourism. 15 Aug. 2008. <http://www.discoversouthcarolina.com/see-do/history-heritage/african_american.aspx?page=7&>.

bathroom. Running behind a tree, I thought that was normal. I thought everybody did that. My parents never told me, 'Son, the reason why we're not stopping at these restaurants is that we're not allowed in there to use that facility.'

"I remember when I must have been seven or eight years old we stopped at a Tasty Twirl. I was consistent and persistent about getting an ice-cream cone.

"'Naw, you don't need an ice-cream cone,' my father said.

"'I want an ice cream cone,' I told my father. I was in line and all the other kids—they were all white—came in front of me and got served. I'm up at the window and I was this little kid trying to figure out why I'm not getting served.

"After about twenty minutes my father just said, 'Son, come on.' and to this day he still didn't tell me why I wasn't served."

RAY NELSON

I received a letter from Ray in which he discusses a woman he met while canvassing for voters near Pineville. This story is what our summer was all about.

"The longer I live and the more I learn, the more I am in awe of the courage and passion of the people we came into contact with. We were part of something begun long before we were born and it will go on, I suppose, when our great-grandchildren are dead.

"Victoria Moultrie lived around Hugar. You remember that you had to sign your name to register to vote, but most of the older ones had never learned. Victoria was an exception. She told us she had learned it as a little girl in school. She said she was ninety-seven.

"That makes her a little girl in the early 1870s. [Victoria] must have started her education in a Freedman's Bureau school. Deke and I were finishing a job that a teacher started ninety years before . . . I have thought about those who helped her, the teacher who taught her and all of those who wanted real freedom for her. They must have been bitterly disappointed at the time. I have thought about all those who have opposed what she did. They must have been very confident. One side had force and power, the weight of opinion and the power of money. But they didn't win. Victoria Moultrie won when she registered to vote in the fall of 1965."

THERESA "CUTIE" SUMPTER

Cutie, eighty-five when I visited her in her home in 2006, did not work on the registration project. But she did have the volunteers over for dinner one Sunday. After a long conversation I asked her if she remembered what she fixed for us for dinner.

"Sure Ah remember what Ah fixed for Sunday dinner for y'all in 1965: fried chicken, butter beans, macaroni and cheese, cake and soda."

"I understand some white man told you not to have civil rights workers over for dinner."

"My husband say that he talked with a white man who told him Ah shouldn' do it. But Ah said Ah can have whoever Ah wants to eat at my house."

"You baked us a cake. How did you do that with a wood stove?"

"[Ah baked cakes in a wood stove and] in the chimney with the iron cross to set the pot. You get the oak wood and burn the oak wood. Then you put a little bit of coals under the bottom of the pot and when that cake done rise up, you put a little of the coals on the top of the pot lid to brown it."

"Sarah Butler taught me how to make sweet potato pie on a wood stove, but I don't remember all of this."

"Ah's got me a good stove now," she says pointing to her kitchen where a gleaming stove sat. I don't know if it was electric or gas.

LUCILLE WASHINGTON

Rebecca Crawford and I corresponded until her death at eighty-three from a stroke in 1993. She usually began, "Dear Sherie, These words leave me feeling good and hoping you is good, too." Since she was unable to write in the summer of 1965. I wonder how she wrote even repetitive letters. Handwriting gave her away. The letters were rarely written by the same hand. As far as I can tell, she never learned to write more than her first name. Lucille Washington, Rebecca Crawford's daughter, was seventy-two in 2005 when I spoke to her.

"Your mother was very courageous," I commented to Lucille.

"Oh, yes, she certainly was."

"But she didn't register to vote because she couldn't write," I said.

"Lord, girl, she done registered. She went to that evenin' school you all started until she could write her last name. As soon as she was able, she registered."

"Really?"

"Oh yes, Mama loved to vote. She 'specially loved to vote for president."

"Hallelujah. It's been forty years and I never knew that."

"She always beat me to vote. And that votin' made a difference. We gots to go to school, to ride the bus and to sit where we want on the bus."

"I didn't know that when I sent you the copy of 'A Line in the Sand.' I'm so proud of her."

Lucille explained that, although poverty and color demanded much, her mother was fiercely independent until Alzheimer's took away her ability to run her own life. She had to move in with Lucille in Charleston. She loved her church and her last job in Charleston working in a flower nursery, but Alzheimer's eventually left her incapable of even boiling rice to feed herself and unable to understand why Lucille had to do so much for her.

Lucille had left her mother behind when she moved to Charleston as soon as she was old enough to escape the daily drudgery of Pineville. She was tired of working in the cotton fields from half light until midmorning when she went to the house to cook the midday meal for the cotton-picking crew. Once they were on their way back to the field, she cleaned up, washed clothes and prepared supper for the evening meal before returning to the field. In Charleston, she worked as a nurse until she married and had seven children of her own.

I asked her why her mother only had three since large families are common in Pineville. She recalled her spunky mama saying, "What do Ah want all them children for?"

Mrs. Crawford was a wandering Alzheimer's patient. Eventually Lucille had to move her into round-the-clock care. Whenever Lucille visited, her mother begged to go home to her blue house on the sandy road. She longed for her home, unable to remember that it was gone.

"Remember you sent me a copy of that certificate you got for writin' Mama's story for that contes'?"

"Yes."

"Well, Ah'm goin' to get a frame and put it on the wall. To think someone wrote a story about my mama. Now that's a gift from God."

9-13-82

Dear Mr and Mrs. Fink -

So nice of you to remember me all the time. I shall never forget your kindness, Thanks a million for the $20.00 again thanks.

Trust your husband continues to improve may God continue His richest Blessing on you both.

I know your trip to Hawaii was much enjoyed. I wish you many more trips (safe)

am attending Senior Citizens program every Day- enjoy it so much. So sorry your car was broken into - But you were so lucky you + John were not hurt

I hope you enjoyed the trip climbing the mountains - and how lucky you were not to have had an accident.

We are having plenty, plenty rain and now you can fall approaching.

will expect to write whenever You can.

Love to each of you
Rebecca Jefferson

This is a letter from Mrs. Crawford. She remarried after 1965. It's addressed to my husband and me.

When I was in Pineville I met many folks over thirty who could neither read nor write. There were many younger folks for whom college was an impossible dream if it was even a passing thought. Education became a priority once voting rights were won.

FORTRENA HASKELL

Fortrena Haskell (Trena) was five in 1965 and her father was the President of the NAACP in Cross, South Carolina, not far from Pineville. Trena went to school and became a legal assistant, legal secretary and paralegal. She's currently an administrative assistant for the Charleston County School District, while studying for her bachelor's degree in business administration. In 2006, Ryan Alston, Fortrena Haskell's son, was a high school senior. He doesn't remember a time when he wasn't expected to go to college.

CORETTA SIMMONS

George and Martha Prioleau Simmons, the owners of the Freedom House and store, had a daughter, Coretta, born in 1966. I didn't meet her until 2006. She graduated with a BA from the University of South Carolina and went on to become a paralegal before receiving a MBA and a Master's in Human Resources Management from Webster University at the Columbia, South Carolina, campus.

I asked her, "So, the idea of having segregated everything was before your time?"

She answered, "I can remember being in maybe the second or third grade; I remember seeing a couple of white students at J. K.—the elementary school. They lived in Russellville and rode a bus. That's probably my first experience. But, I had a white teacher's assistant in kindergarten and then mother had a local woman, a white lady, to teach me piano lessons. When her father-in-law found out that she was teaching me, she had to stop."

ONTARIO SMALLS

Ontario and Chequetta Smalls are a young married couple with two children, one of elementary school age. During the summer of 1965, I met his great-grandmother, Sarah Butler. She was able to read and write and had registered to vote, though her husband refused to learn to read. When I went "home" from Allen University for Thanksgiving and Christmas, I stayed with the Butlers and my connection with the Butler family has deepened over time. Ontario and Chequetta's daughter is going to a progressive, award-winning elementary school in Atlanta, Georgia. They realize that her success in school starts at the very beginning!

DEBORAH WILLIAMS

Deborah was one of the skinny little girls leaving Mrs. Simmons's store the day we arrived. She was ten and lived across the road from the Freedom House. Today her daughter has a Master's Degree in Rehabilitation Counseling. Her son will graduate from high school this year, "My son is going to college!" Deborah tells me she graduated from Limestone College in Gaffney, South Carolina, in December of 2007 with a degree in social work, having entered college after her children were out of high school.

APPENDIX C

The Art of Nourishment

I remember clearly that at the Atlanta orientation the staff attempted to give us an inkling of issues that would arise because we were entering a different culture. When asked what to expect for food in our new surroundings, Reverend Andrew Young summed it up in two words: "Eat it." The following is a discussion I enjoyed very much and it illustrates the point that these people were poor, that food was scarce, and that people made ends meet in "interesting" ways.

This conversation took place at Cutie's house. We were all sitting around talking about food in 1965 and today. Present at this discussion are Cutie (85), Lottie Smalls (85), and Shirley Farness (69). All three women are lifelong Pineville citizens.

Cutie said, "People shared more in 1965. People raised they own hogs, they own chickens, they own eggs. If one kill a hog, everybody goin' to get a taste then."

"Thas right," Lottie echoed.

"Now the chilren they don't want no hog, don't want no chicken out the yard, don't want the egg or nothing . . . And there's nothing better to eat than coon."

"Yes, Lord," Lottie said.

"That squirrel is good and the rabbit and the deer. That was our meat, and the fish, too."

"Ah don't want the coon either and the squirrel either and the deer either. No, ma'am. If they don't sell it in the store, Ah don't eat it," Shirley offered.

"What always hurt my heart," Lottie declared, "was what do you say to your chilren when theys still hungry after they eat and theys no more food to give 'em?"

⌐⌐

Later, at Lottie's house, the subject came up again.

I asked Albertha Butler (79), Lottie's sister-in-law, if she was the person who taught me to put just a touch of sugar in the flour before dredging my pork chops to add to the flavor?

"It surely wasn't me," Albertha said. "We didn't have sugar to waste that way. The kids would eat sugar when Ah was out the house. They tried to clean it up but they couldn't all the way. Ah always knew."

Lottie commented, "We didn't always have enough to eat."

"Ah know what you're talking about," Albertha continued. "Before we'd go to the field in the mornin', Ah left a sweet potato in the ashes in the chimney. Ah'd dig in the ashes for that sweet potato, all Ah ate for lunch."

Noel, Lottie's daughter (57) added, ""Jerome ate possum, but Ah'd rather not eat than eat it." (Jerome is her older brother.)

My favorite remark is, "Ah ate possum until Ah was coming home through the cemetery and saw a possum chewing on something it pulled out of a new grave. Ah don't eat possum anymore." Unfortunately I don't remember who said it.

APPENDIX D

SCLC Orientation

SCLC planned a week of intense lectures, workshops, singing, and movies. This is the schedule for the first day. The other days follow.

```
                        The SCOPE of Freedom:
        The Leadership of Hosea Williams with Dr. King's Summer '65 Student Volunteers

                            AGENDA

                      ORIENTATION SESSION

              SOUTHERN CHRISTIAN LEADERSHIP CONFERENCE

          SUMMER COMMUNITY ORGANIZATION POLITICAL EDUCATION

                            (SCOPE)

                                        June 14 - 19, 1965

        Hosea L. Williams, Director
        SCLC - SCOPE
        Bayard Rustin, Executive Director
        A. Philip Randolph Institute;
        Orientation Program Director
        Norman Hill, Industrial Union Department,
        AFL-CIO; Associate Director, Orientation Program



                        Monday, June 14

        8 - 9 A.M.                   Breakfast

        9 - 10 A.M.                  Free Time

        10 - 11 A.M.                 Plenary Session
                                     "History of SCLC," by The Reverend
                                     Ralph D. Abernathy, Vice-President
                                     at large and Treasurer, SCLC

                                     "Why We Are Here," by Hosea L.
                                     Williams, SCOPE Director

        11A.M.- 12 P.M.              Report of Student Orientation Policy
                                     Committee.
                                     Report Discussion: Questions and
                                     general announcements.

        12:30 - 1:30                 Lunch

        1:30 - 2 P.M.                Free Time

        2 - 3 P.M.                   Plenary Session
                                     "The Civil Rights Movement since 1954,"
                                     "History and Perspectives," by Bayard Rustin

                            (continued)
```

Appendix D: SCLC Orientation

3 - 4 P.M.　　　　　　　Workshops on Mr. Rustin's address
　　　　　　　　　　　　conducted by SCLC Staffers and
　　　　　　　　　　　　assigned faculty members.

4 - 6 P.M.　　　　　　　Symposia: These sessions are designed
　　　　　　　　　　　　for discussions and questions on any
　　　　　　　　　　　　subject by students

6:30 - 7 P.M.　　　　　　Dinner

7 - 8 P.M.　　　　　　　"Why We Are Here," by Dr. Martin
　　　　　　　　　　　　Luther King, Jr.

8 - 9 P.M.　　　　　　　Plenary Session
　　　　　　　　　　　　"The Civil Rights Act of 1964," address
　　　　　　　　　　　　by Joseph Rauh, Counsel, Leadership
　　　　　　　　　　　　Conference on Civil Rights
　　　　　　　　　　　　Commentator: The Reverend Walter E.
　　　　　　　　　　　　Fauntroy, Director - Washington Office

9 - 10:30 P.M.　　　　　Workshops on implementation of The
　　　　　　　　　　　　Civil Rights Bill of 1964," conducted
　　　　　　　　　　　　by SCLC Staffers, members of the U. S.
　　　　　　　　　　　　Civil Rights Commission, and Staff of
　　　　　　　　　　　　The NAACP Legal Defense Fund, Inc.

10:30　　　　　　　　　Songfest: Freedom songs, Folksongs, et
　　　　　　　　　　　　conducted by Mrs. Septima P. Clark,
　　　　　　　　　　　　Supervisor Teacher Training, Citizenship
　　　　　　　　　　　　Education Program, SCLC

(Note: During the Symposia period, 4 - 6 P.M., those persons particularl
interested in literacy training will meet with Mrs. Septima Clark and Dr.
Theodore Pinnock of Tuskegee Institute. Tuskegee, Alabama.)

\#\#\#\#\#\#\#\#\#\#

283

~ 154 ~

The SCOPE of Freedom:

The Leadership of Hosea Williams with Dr. King's Summer '65 Student Volunteers

TUESDAY, June 15

SCLC - SCOPE Agenda Orientation

8 - 9 A.M.	Breakfast
9 - 10 A.M.	Free Time
10 - 11 A.M.	Plenary Session "The Meaning and Relevance of Nonviolence," The Reverend James Lawson, Director, Nonviolent Education Commentators: Dr. King, Bayard Rustin, Reverend Andrew Young and others.
11 - 12:30 P.M.	Workshops on the theory and practice of nonviolent resistance conducted by SCLC Staffers and assigned faculty members.
12:30 - 1:30 P.M.	Lunch
1:30 P.M.	News Conference (place to be announced) Dr. King, SCLC President and selected Orientation Officials.
1:30 - 2:30 P.M.	Free Time
2 - 3 P.M.	Plenary Session "The Relationship of Southern History to the Negro Revolution," address by C. Vann Woodard, American History Professor, Yale University Commentator: August Meier, American History Professor, Roosevelt University, Chicago, Illinois
3 - 4 P.M.	Workshops on Southern History conducted by SCLC Staffers and assigned faculty.
4 - 6 P.M.	Extended workshops and symposia
6 - 7 P.M.	Dinner
7 - 8 P.M.	Free Time

(continued)

Tuesday's Agenda - Page 2

8 - 9 P.M.   Plenary Session
                              "Farm Labor in the South," address by
                              Jac Wasserman, Representative of The
                              U. S. Dept. of Agriculture, Director,
                              Atlanta Office, National Sharecroppers
                              Fund.

9 - 10 P.M.   Workshops on farm labor, with emphasis
                              on available government loans, assistance
                              and local farm boards; conducted by the
                              National Sharecroppers Fund Staff and the
                              U. S. Civil Rights Commission.

10 P.M.   Film: "Right Now," "The Mississippi
                              Story;" Freedom Songs.

###############

285

WEDNESDAY, June 16

SCLC – SCOPE Agenda Orientation

8 – 9 A.M.	Breakfast
9 – 10 A.M.	Free Time
10 – 11 A.M.	Plenary Session "National Implications of the Southern Movement," James Bevel, Director, Direct Action, SCLC and Michael Harrington, author, "Other America" and chairman of the board, League for Industrial Democracy (LID) Commentator: Tom Kahn, Executive Secretary, LID
11 A.M. – 12:30 P.M.	Workshops on Mr. Harrington's talk; conducted by SCLC Staffers and assigned faculty members.
12:30 – 1:30 P.M.	Lunch
1:30 – 2 P.M.	Free Time
2 – 3 P.M.	Plenary Session "The War on Poverty in the South," Brendan Sexton, Office of Economic Opportunity (OEO) Commentator: Vernon Jordan, Atlanta Office, OEO
3 – 4 P.M.	Workshops on the use of the War on Poverty in specific areas; conducted by staff of the Office of Economic Opportunity and assigned faculty members.
4 – 6 P.M.	Symposia
6 – 7 P.M.	Dinner
7 – 7:30 P.M.	Free Time
7:30 – 8:30 P.M.	Plenary Session "Community Organization," panel composed of SCLC Staffers, chaired by Randolph T. Blackwell, Program Director, SCLC, and Hosea L. Williams, with the assistance of grass roots persons from black belt counties.

(continued)

286

The SCOPE of Freedom:

The Leadership of Hosea Williams with Dr. King's Summer '65 Student Volunteers

Wednesday's Agenda – Page 2

8:30 – 9 P.M.   A discussion of medical problems by Dr. William Stewart, Medical Committee for Human Rights.

9 – 10 P.M.   Workshops to cover specific areas under community organization, conducted by SCLC Staffers and assigned faculty.

(Note: During workshops on poverty, 3 – 4 P.M., persons particularly interested in agricultural problems will meet with a representative of the Department of Agriculture.)

###############

The SCOPE of Freedom:

The Leadership of Hosea Williams with Dr. King's Summer '65 Student Volunteers

THURSDAY, June 17

SCLC - SCOPE Agenda Orientation

8 - 9 A.M.	Breakfast
9 - 10 A.M.	Free Time
10 - 11 A.M.	Plenary Session "The Labor Movement in the South," Donald Slaiman, Director, Civil Rights Department, AFL-CIO
11 A.M. - 12 P.M.	Workshops on Mr. Slaiman's address with emphasis on basic problems of local com- munities - - specific people to talk to in local areas, how to relate to the local AFL-CIO, when to contact the National Committee on Political Education (COPE); Norman Hill, Industrial Union Department; AFL-CIO; Al Kehrer, AFL-CIO Civil Rights Department, Cleveland Robinson, Secretary- Treasurer, District 65, RWDSU
12 - 12:30 P.M.	Free Time
12:30 - 1:30 P.M.	Lunch
1:30 - 2 P.M.	Free Time
2 - 3 P.M.	Plenary Session "Title VII: Federal Fair Employment Practices Act," address by LeRoy Clark, NAACP Legal Defense Fund
3 - 3:30 P.M.	"The Challenge to You," by Reverend C. T. Vivian, Affiliate Director, SCLC
3:30 - 5:30 P.M.	County assignments: Discussions and questions, Hosea Williams and SCLC Staffers
5:30 - 6 P.M.	Free Time
6 - 7 P.M.	Dinner
7 - 8 P.M.	"The Dynamics That Led to the Civil Rights Act of 1964 and The Voting Bill of 1965;" The Reverend Andrew Young, Executive Director, SCLC.

(continued)

The SCOPE of Freedom:
The Leadership of Hosea Williams with Dr. King's Summer '65 Student Volunteers

Thursday's Agenda - Page 2

8 - 9 P.M. Plenary Session
"The Voting Bill of 1965: Its Affect on the
Deep South," by Clarence Mitchell,
Director, Washington Bureau, NAACP;
session chaired by Dr. King

9 - 10 P.M. Workshops on voter registration, canvassing, suggestions, etc., conducted
by SCLC Staffers, COPE Staff, and assigned
faculty members.

10 P.M. Film: "Nothing But A Man" - Freedom Songs.

###############

The SCOPE of Freedom:

The Leadership of Hosea Williams with Dr. King's Summer '65 Student Volunteers

SCLC - SCOPE Agenda Orientation

8 - 9 A.M.	Breakfast
9 - 10 A.M.	Free Time
10 - 11 A.M.	Plenary Session "Problems of Understanding: North, South, Black, White," by Dr. John Morsell, Assistant Executive Director, NAACP
	Commentators: Harry Boyte, The Reverend Andrew J. Young and Dorothy Cotton.
11 A.M. - 12 Noon	Workshops on Negro-white staff relations, relations with people in the counties, etc., conducted by SCLC Staffers and assigned faculty members.
12 Noon - 12:30 P.M.	Free Time
12:30 - 1:30 P.M.	Lunch
1:30 - 2 P.M.	Free Time
2 - 3 P.M.	Plenary Session "The South and The Law," by Jack Greenberg, Director, NAACP Legal Defense and Education Fund.
3 - 4 P.M.	Workshops on what to do when arrested, when in court, without a lawyer, how to contact the Justice Department, etc., conducted by Charles Morgan, Southern Director, ACLU, Norm Amaker, Staff NAACP Legal Defense Fund, Don Hollowell, Hon. LeRoy Johnson, State Senator, Georgia.
4 - 6 P.M.	Free Time
6 - 7 P.M.	Dinner
7 - 7:30 P.M.	Free Time
8:30 P.M.	"Contribution of the Civil Rights Revolution to American Democracy," by Ralph Helstein, President, United Packinghouse Workers of America, AFL-CIO, chaired by Dr. King

The SCOPE of Freedom:
The Leadership of Hosea Williams with Dr. King's Summer '65 Student Volunteers

SATURDAY, June 19

SCLC - SCOPE Agenda Orientation

(Flexible Day - Agenda to be determined by SCLC Staffers and Student Committee)

A.   1) How to hold a mass meeting

    2) Press Relations - Junius Griffin, SCLC, Public Relations Staffer

    3) Use of WATS Line

    4) Contacting Congressmen and local papers - Mississippi Challenge

    5) Relationship of volunteers to local projects, field staff, and SCLC National Office

    6) Relations with Northern Groups

B.   Break up into county groups to discuss specific plans

1 P. M.   ADJOURNMENT

APPENDIX E

SCLC Evaluation

After the summer project, SCLC asked participants to evaluate their experiences. Below is my evaluation.

APPENDIX F

SCLC Reading List

After we were accepted as participants, SCLC sent us this reading list. My partial reading list is on page 166.

SUGGESTED READING MATERIAL FOR SCOPE WORKERS
563 Johnson Avenue, N.E.
Atlanta, Georgia 30303
Telephone 522-2023 (404)

1. C. Vann Woodward, "From the First Reconstruction To The Second," Harper's
   April, 1965   (Must get permission to reprint from
                        John Fischer. Editor, Harper's Magazine,
                        49 East 33rd Street, New York 10016)

2. Louis Lomax, "Georgia Boy Goes Home", Harper's, April, 1965
                        (Same as above on permission)

3. Erwin Knoll, "Ten Years of Deliberate Speed", American Education, Vol. 1,
   Number 1, Dec. 1964-Jan.1965. This is published by U.S. Office
   of Education, Washington, D.C. It is in the public domain--
   so no permission necessary. Call John Naisbitt, U.S. Office of
   Education, for copies.

4. Luther Foster, "The American Negro in Transition: An Overview", Michigan
   Quarterly Review, Jan. 1965. President Foster of Tuskegee
   Institute has reprints. Ask him for them.

5. How To Win, AFL-CIO Committee on Political Education, AFL-CIO Building, 815
   16th Street, N.W., Washington, D.C. (PB). (Handbook on political
   organization, voter registration,etc.

6. "Mandate for the Great Society", by Herman Edelsberg, The ADL Bulletin, Dec.
   1964. Can be had free from Anti-Defamation League of B'nai B'rith,
   315 Lexington Avenue, New York City (Write them for copies)

7. Arnold Rose, "Social Change and the Negro Problem", ADL pamphlet, 1964.
   Again write Anti-Defamation League in NYC and get copies.

8. Kenneth B. Clark, "Delusions of the White Liberal", New York Times Magazine.
   April 4, 1965.

                  (Permission has to be given by the N.Y. Times. Write Lester
                  Markel, N.Y. Times. Times Square, N.Y.)

9. Ernest Dunbar, "The Negro in America Today", Look, April 10, 1962.

10. Robert Penn Warren, "The Negro Now", Look, March 23, 1965.
                  (Permission has to be given by Look to use these. Write
                  Leo Rosten. Look Magazine, 488 Madison Avenue, New York City)

MY PARTIAL READING LIST FROM 1965

Cash, W.J. *The Mind of the South*

Dollard, John. *Caste and Class in a Southern Town*

Douglass, Frederick. A *Narrative on the Life of Frederick Douglass, an American Slave*

DuBois, W.E.B. *Souls of Black Folk*

Baldwin, James. *Another Country*

————. *The Fire Next Time*

————. *Giovanni's Room*

————. *Go Tell It on the Mountain*

Gregory, Dick. *From the Back of the Bus*

Griffin, John Howard. *Black Like Me*

King, Dr. Martin Luther, Jr. *Strength to Love*

————. *Why We Can't Wait*

Lomax, Louis E. *The Negro Revolt*

McKitrick, Eric L. *Slavery Defended: the Views of the Old South*

Smith, Lillian. *Killers of the Dream*

Stamp, Kenneth. *The Peculiar Institution*

Woodward, C. Vann. *The Strange Career of Jim Crow*

APPENDIX G

Resolution Passed at the Death of
Mrs. Martha Ann Middleton Prioleau Simmons

Resolution Passed at the Death of
Mrs. Martha Ann Middleton Prioleau Simmons

South Carolina General Assembly
117th Session, 2007-2008

H. 4026

STATUS INFORMATION

Concurrent Resolution
Sponsors: Reps. Jefferson, Williams, Agnew, Alexander, Allen, Anderson, Anthony, Bales, Ballentine, Bannister, Barfield, Battle, Bedingfield, Bingham, Bowen, Bowers, Brady, Branham, Brantley, Breeland, G. Brown, R. Brown, Cato, Ceips, Chalk, Chellis, Clemmons, Clyburn, Cobb-Hunter, Coleman, Cooper, Cotty, Crawford, Dantzler, Davenport, Delleney, Duncan, Edge, Frye, Funderburk, Gambrell, Govan, Gullick, Hagood, Haley, Hamilton, Hardwick, Harrell, Harrison, Hart, Harvin, Haskins, Hayes, Herbkersman, Hinson, Hiott, Hodges, Hosey, Howard, Huggins, Jennings, Kelly, Kennedy, Kirsh, Knight, Leach, Limehouse, Littlejohn, Loftis, Lowe, Lucas, Mack, Mahaffey, McLeod, Merrill, Miller, Mitchell, Moody-Lawrence, Moss, Mulvaney, J.H. Neal, J.M. Neal, Neilson, Ott, Owens, Parks, Perry, Phillips, Pinson, E.H. Pitts, M.A. Pitts, Rice, Rutherford, Sandifer, Scarborough, Scott, Sellers, Shoopman, Simrill, Skelton, D.C. Smith, F.N. Smith, G.M. Smith, G.R. Smith, J.E. Smith, J.R. Smith, W.D. Smith, Spires, Stavrinakis, Stewart, Talley, Taylor, Thompson, Toole, Umphlett, Vick, Viers, Walker, Weeks, Whipper, White, Whitmire, Witherspoon and Young
Document Path: l:\council\bills\bbm\10026htc07.doc

Introduced in the House on May 2, 2007
Introduced in the Senate on May 2, 2007
Adopted by the General Assembly on May 2, 2007

Summary: Martha Ann Middleton Prioleau Simmons

HISTORY OF LEGISLATIVE ACTIONS

Date	Body	Action Description with journal page number
5/2/2007	House	Introduced, adopted, sent to Senate HJ-68
5/2/2007	Senate	Introduced, adopted, returned with concurrence SJ-12

A CONCURRENT RESOLUTION

EXPRESSING THE SYMPATHY OF THE MEMBERS OF THE GENERAL ASSEMBLY TO THE FAMILY AND MANY FRIENDS OF THE LATE MARTHA ANN MIDDLETON PRIOLEAU SIMMONS OF PINEVILLE IN BERKELEY COUNTY.

Whereas, the members of the General Assembly were saddened to note the passing on October 22, 2006, of Martha Ann Middleton Prioleau Simmons of Pineville, in Berkeley County; and

Whereas, Martha Ann Middleton Prioleau Simmons, born March 13, 1913, was the seventh child of Artopee Middleton and Celia Mariah Lloyd Middleton and was the last surviving offspring of ten daughters born to this union; and

Whereas, she began her formal education in the public schools of Berkeley County by attending Crawl Creek School and Mall School, now known as J. K. Gourdin, continuing on to Avery Institute in Charleston, Voorhees College, and South Carolina State College; and

Whereas, she started and taught "The One-Room Classroom" elementary school in the Judgetown section of Pineville; and

Whereas, she was a communicate member of Redeemer Reformed Episcopal Church in Pineville, singing in the Youth Choir and later the Adult Choir, and ultimately the Senior Choir, serving also as church secretary to the Vestry, teaching the Cradle Roll Sunday School Class, working with the Women of the Church Auxiliary, serving as chairperson of many programs sponsored by the church, and representing the church as a delegate at denomination convocations; and

Whereas, while attending college she worked at the cigar factory and as a welder at the Naval Shipyard in Charleston. She also worked with North Carolina Mutual Insurance Company for nearly twenty years and she later drove school buses for the Berkeley County School System, while serving as a librarian at St. Stephen High School; and

Whereas, Ms. Simmons was the last surviving charter (founding) member of St. John Chapter #213, Order of the Eastern Star, Pineville Chapter, and served as its first Worthy Matron; and

Whereas, in 1940, she married Elijah Prioleau, and this union was blessed with three children. After her husband's death in 1963, she continued to manage and operate the family grocery store in Pineville. In 1964, she began operating a daycare center in the back of the store and notably, eighty percent of those students went on to become college graduates; and

Whereas, in 1965, she married George Simmons, who also preceded her in death. This union was blessed with two daughters; and

Whereas, she was a pioneer of her time; active in civil rights causes, believing in justice and equal treatment for all mankind and working toward wiping out discrimination and prejudices in our society. She was not afraid to venture into unchartered territory acting to facilitate in voter registration efforts and rural healthcare; and

Whereas, during the summers of 1974 and 1975, she pioneered a summer youth work program in which she offered employment opportunities to teens at her daycare center, which ultimately became known as the Berkeley County Citizens' Day Care Center, and managing and operating the center until the onset of declining health; and

Whereas, she was a woman of strong Christian faith, continually trusting and believing that God would always make a way. And it became known to all who knew her that Psalm 37 was her favorite book in the Holy Bible, and the 25th verse was her favorite; and

Whereas, it is appropriate for the members of the General Assembly to pause in their deliberations so that they might honor the memory of such a great a daughter of South Carolina. Now, therefore,

Be it resolved by the House of Representatives, the Senate concurring:

That the members of the General Assembly, by this resolution, express their sympathy to the family and many friends of the late Martha Ann Middleton Prioleau Simmons of Pineville in Berkeley County.

Be it further resolved that a copy of this resolution be forwarded to the beloved children of Martha Ann Middleton Prioleau Simmons, Jerrous "Jerry" Prioleau, Derrous "Dee" P. Cameron, Patricia M. (L.C.) Sanders, Oswald Reginald "Reggie" (Mildred) Prioleau, and Coretta Simmons.

----XX----

APPENDIX H

The Right to Vote

A n ex-student of mine wrote me, "I'm an American . . . I have the freedom to not give a crap enough to vote, and the right to complain long and loud about the guy that gets elected." I think of Rebecca Crawford, Martha Prioleau Simmons, the congregation of Redeemer Reformed Episcopal Church and other members of the Pineville community. How would they respond to this attitude?

The people of Pineville understood the power of the vote and were willing to struggle for it. Americans love to complain. But so many of us feel it's passé to be a dutiful and responsible citizen. We are all familiar with our rights, but many of us feel our personal entitlement is the reason this country exists—a free pass to do whatever we want to. I think that attitude is part of the reason the United States is in such a dire situation. Too many Americans have decided democracy is just about them and so they quit participating.

The Founding Fathers limited voting to white men who owned property, paid taxes and (in all thirteen colonies) believed in God. Most of the people who fit this category were also educated and felt a responsibility to their new government because they had fought a war to earn it. Their participation was a patriotic duty.

They also wanted to protect the country from elected officials who would take advantage of their power. After they'd fought a war where Americans died for the right to vote they devised an extraordinary document which provided separation of powers, checks and balances, and separation of church and state—our Constitution. A purpose of this document: *to make sure that no one took advantage of their elected position.*

The history of America since then has been a struggle by other groups to gain the right and privilege to vote and support the Constitution. Most white male citizens earned the right to vote during the time of President Jackson (1829-1837) when it was more important to be a good shot and capable woodsman than it was to own property. As a result of the Civil War (1861-1865), black men got the right to vote, although it took the Civil Rights Movement of the 1950's and1960's to make that promise a reality. Women didn't get the right to vote until the Nineteenth Amendment (1920).

Voting used to be important. What went wrong? There is a popular phrase, "If you like your freedom, thank a veteran." And it applies to all of those men and women who died trying to protect the Constitution and the country built upon it. It seems to me that voting would be such an important privilege that we'd have a ninety-five percent turnout for every election.

However, the national statistics from 1960 to 2008 show how unimportant voting is to those of us who appreciate the Founding Fathers and revere our servicemen and women's sacrifice. The highest percentage of voters participating after 1960 was 61.9% in 1964. The lowest turnout: 36.4% in 1998. The new century didn't prompt us to vote:

2008	<u>56.8%</u>
2006	37.1%
2004	<u>55.3%</u>
2002	37.0%
2000	<u>51.3%</u>

(The underlined percentages are years when presidents, senators and representatives are elected. The others are interim elections where only senators and members of the House of Representatives are elected.)

If our elected officials are not doing the job we want them to do, it's because we have given them carte blanche to wield their power without limitations. We don't use the most basic tool of a democracy: voting. If politicians have become as "evil" as some folks believe, it's because we turned them loose and then refused to do anything more than whine. It's time for us to take back the power the Founding Fathers gave us: the right to vote. Perhaps, Mrs. Simmons and Mrs. Crawford would point out that all we have to do is talk to voters one at a time until they understand how important they are.

BIBLIOGRAPHY

Alim, H. Samy and Baugh, John, eds. *Talkin' Black Talk.* New York: Teachers College Press., 2007.

Belfrage, Sally. *Freedom Summer.* New York: Fawcett Publications, 1965.

Brewer, Holly. *Women in Colonial America.* North Carolina State University. 10 Apr. 2008. <www.dlt.ncssm.edu/lmtm/docs/women_col_am/script.pdf >.

Due, Tananarive and Due, Patricia Stephens. *Freedom in the Family: A Mother-Daughter Memoir of the Fight for Civil Rights.* New York: Ballantine Books, 2003.

Edgar, Walter (editor). *South Carolina Encyclopedia.* Columbia: University of South Carolina Press. 2006.

The Free Dictionary by Farlex. 5 June 2008. <http://www.thefreedictionary.com/juke>.

Ginzburg, Ralph. *100 Years of Lynchings.* Baltimore: Black Classic Press, 1988.

House Bill 4026. South Carolina General Assembly. 2 May 2007. <http://www.scstatehouse.gov/sess117_2007-2008/bills/4026.htm>.

Katz, William L. Katz. *Eyewitness: the Negro in American History.* New York: Pitman Publishing Corporation, 1967.

Labedis, Sherie. Journal: Summer, 1965.

"The Language of the Sea Islands." Gullah Heritage: the Language of the Sea Islands. 4 Aug. 2010. <http://www.islandpacket.com/man/gullah/language.html>.

Leventhal, Willy Siegel. *The SCOPE of Freedom: The Leadership of Hosea Williams with Dr. King's Summer '65 Student Volunteers.* Montgomery: Challenge Publishing. 2005.

National Voter Turnout in Federal Elections: 1960-2008. Infoplease. com 4 June, <2010. http://www.infoplease.com/ipa/A0781453. html#axzz0ymqsxbua>.

Manuscript of the trial of the State of South Carolina vs. Barrett, Bryant, Kennedy, Nelson, Lawlor, Frasier, Saunders [sic], Gallashaw, Bennett, Miroff, Tenbrink, Williams and Daniels. 1965.

McAdam, Doug. *Freedom Summer.* New York: Oxford University Press, 1988.

Montgomery, Warner M. "Pineville: A Historic Refuge." *Columbia Star.* Jan. 18, 2008.

Moody, Anne. *Coming of Age in Mississippi.* New York: Laurel Books, 1968.

Moore, Winfred B. and Burton, Orville Vernon, eds. *Toward the Meeting of the Waters: Currents in the Civil Rights Movement of South Carolina During the Twentieth Century.* Columbia: University of South Carolina Press, 2008.

Mufwene, Salikoko S., Rickford, John R., Bailey, Guy, and Baugh, John. *African-American English Structure, History and Usage.* London: Routledge, 1998.

Nash, Gary B. American *Odyssey: The United States in the Twentieth Century.* New York: Glenco. 1997.

The New Oxford American Dictionary. New York: Oxford University Press, Inc., 2005.

Norton, Mary Beth, Katzman, David M., Escott, Paul D., Chudacoff, Howard P., Paterson, Thomas G. and Tuttle, William M., Jr. *People and a Nation: History of the United States.* Boston: Houghton Mifflin, 1986.

The Official Tourism Site of the State of South Carolina. South Carolina Department of Parks, Recreation & Tourism. 15 Aug. 2008. <http://www.discoversouthcarolina.com/products/3671.aspx>.

Rickford, John Russell. *African American Vernacular English: Features, Evolution, Educational Implications* (Language in Society). Wiley-Blackwell. 1999.

Rickford, John Russell and Rickford, Russell John. *Spoken Soul: The Story of Black English.* New York: Wiley & Sons, Inc., 2000.

South Carolina Department of Archives and History. 9 Feb. 2008. <http://www.nationalregister.sc.gov/berkeley/S10817708014/index. htm>.

Thomas, Velma Maia. *We Shall Not be Moved: The Passage from the Great Migration to the Million Man March.* New York: Crown Publishers, Inc., 2002.

Turner, Lorenzo Dow, Mille, Katherine Wyly and Montgomery, Michael B. *Africanisms in the Gullah Dialect.* Columbia: University of South Carolina Press, 2002.

CREDITS

I am indebted to Nellie Habegger, Carol Sanders Hanig and Julie TenBrink for most of the snapshots in this book.

The picture of Redeemer Reformed Episcopal Church came from Alfredia Doiley at the Diocese of the Southeast of the Reformed Episcopal Church.

Coretta Simmons allowed me to publish the "Resolution Passed at the Death of Mrs. Martha Ann Middleton Prioleau Simmons."

The Atlanta Inquirer provided the picture of James Bevel speaking to the volunteers at the SCOPE orientation.

Willy Siegel Leventhal wrote *The SCOPE of Freedom: The Leadership of Hosea Williams with Dr. King's Summer '65 Student Volunteers.* This is where I found the agenda for the orientation, the list of books we were to read before arriving in Atlanta and a copy of my evaluation of the SCOPE project.

Jennifer Gong of Viking Press, Oakmont High School, prepared the maps used in the book.

ABOUT THE AUTHOR

SHERIE LABEDIS was born in Los Angeles, California, in 1946. When she was ten her family moved to rural Shingle Springs, California, where she discovered a passion for civil rights when high school English teacher Bruce Harvey asked his students what they were willing to die for.

"I was galvanized by an address by Dr. Martin Luther King, Jr.," she says today. "Meeting him was the most influential event of my life."

Sherie was only eighteen when she participated in 1965's Summer Community Organization and Political Education project registering black voters in Pineville, South Carolina, for Dr. King's Southern Christian Leadership Conference.

At the end of the summer of 1965, with the financial support of the NAACP, she enrolled for a semester at Allen University, an African Methodist Episcopal college in Columbia, South Carolina. Labedis was the only white student on campus. She returned to the University of California, Berkeley where she earned a bachelor's degree and teaching credential.

She taught history and English for thirty-five years, most of it with at-risk youth, before retiring to write *You Came Here to Die, Didn't You* —her first book.

Sherie lives in Roseville, California, with her husband, Joe, and their dog, Zoë.

She is available for readings of her book, book signings, seminars, and presentations. She can be contacted online at www.sherielabedis.com

INDEX

A

Abernathy, Ralph 9
Abraham 36, 142
Alabama vii, xiv, 12, 14, 32, 34,
    106, 123, 133
Alfonso 142
Allen University in Columbia,
    South Carolina 122, 124, 150
Atlanta, Georgia xvii, 1, 150

B

Bennett's Restaurant 86, 101
Berkeley County, South Carolina
    xv–xvi, 29–31, 35, 40, 82, 127,
    142, 144, 168–169
Berkeley Restaurant 99–101, 113,
    115, 118
Bevel, James 7, 179
"black belt" county 33
Black Volunteers from Berkeley
    County, South Carolina 142
    Abraham 36, 142
    Alfonso 142
    Bryant, Louis (Lefty) 83, 86,
        92, 94–102, 108, 113, 118–
        119, 124, 127, 133, 142
    Darby, Linda Ann 53, 109,
        133, 138, 142
    Gilliard, Azell 142

Laurence 52–54, 142
Lloyd, Beatrice 142
Middleton, Willie, Reverend
    108, 114, 116, 121, 142
Mitchell, Herbert 41, 83, 133,
    138, 142
Moultrie, Henry 41, 142
Prioleau, Ishmael, Jr. 70–76,
    130, 138, 142
Prioleau, Willie Louis 120, 142
Ravenell, Maxine 52, 133, 142
Ravenell, Roger 142
Rose, Doris 55, 116, 142
Simmons, George 121, 127,
    142, 168
Simmons, Lula Mae 52, 133,
    138, 142
Simmons, Martha Ann Middle-
    ton Prioleau xi, 34, 35, 142,
    149, 167–169, 171
Summers, James (Butch) 83,
    138, 142
Swinton, Joe 41, 142
Vaughn 142
Walter 112, 142
Washington, Kenny 41, 109,
    113, 115, 142
White, Deke (Leon) 55–59,
    83, 108, 137, 139, 142, 145
Bobbit, Roger 104
Brown, Russell 61

Brown vs. Board of Education 54
Bryant, Louis (Lefty) 83, 86, 92,
   94–102, 108, 113, 118–119,
   124, 127, 133, 142
Butler, Albertha 138, 152
Butler, Henry 143
Butler, Sarah 146, 150

C

Central High School, Little Rock,
   Arkansas 54
Charleston, South Carolina 16–18,
   21, 24, 26, 29–35, 42, 50–51,
   56, 60–62, 68, 84–85, 107–108,
   112, 116, 127, 134, 141–142,
   147, 149, 168
Civil Rights Act of 1964 7–8, 53,
   117
Civil Rights Act of 1965 54, 116
Civil Rights Movement, The xiv,
   xvii, 1, 3, 5, 8, 10–11, 28, 44,
   51, 106, 108, 123, 172, 176
civil rights worker(s) xvi, 9, 12, 27,
   32, 61, 81, 85, 99, 104, 115,
   146
Civil War, The 33, 172
Congress of Racial Equality 14
Rebecca Crawford 78–79, 82, 110,
   146, 171, 173

D

Darby, Linda Ann 53, 109, 133,
   138, 142
Dennis, Rembert C. 40
desegregation 60, 127, 133
DuBois, W.E.B. 19

E

Edisto Beach 50, 61
Eisenhower, Dwight D., President
   54

F

Farness, Shirley 151
Fashion, David 41
Federal Bureau of Investigation
   (FBI) 115, 131
Fielding, Bernard 61
Folly Beach 60
Freedman's Bureau school 145
Freedom House x, xvi, 12, 35, 38,
   56, 58, 68, 70, 72, 83–84, 86,
   97–100, 103, 108, 112–113,
   134, 141, 149–150
Freedom School 23, 41
freedom songs xv, 5, , 68, 93

G

Gadsden, Abraham, Reverend 41,
   88–89, 104
Gadsden, Bobby 52–53, 94, 96–97,
   113, 142
GeeChee xvi
Gilliard, Azell 98–100, 142
Gullah xvi, 175, 177

H

Habegger, Nellie xvi–xviii, 16–20,
   24, 27–32, 36, 39, 46, 49, 52,
   61, 67–69, 72, 82, 97, 99–100,
   103–104, 107, 121–123, 132,
   138, 141, 179

Harvey, Bruce xiii–xiv
Haskell, Fortrena 138, 149
Haskell, Fortune 41
Head Start 24, 124, 142
Herd, Ron, II xiii
Hickory Hill Baptist Church 47
Holman, Mr. 40
Howard's Restaurant 92–93, 95,
 99, 113, 115–116, 117–119,
 122
Hutchings, Phil xvii

I

illiteracy xv, 7

J

Jefferson, Joseph H. 138, 144
Jenkins, Esau 18, 24, 50
Johnson, Lyndon B., President 8
Jones, Florence xvi, 16–19, 23–25,
 29–34, 37, 39, 40–44, 46,
 50–51, 61–65, 68, 71, 81–82,
 85, 92–93, 99–102, 107–108,
 110, 117–118, 127, 141
J. K. Gourdin Elementary School
 86–88, 168

K

Kennedy, Joan 41, 50, 52, 107,
 141
Kimball, John xvi, 16, 29–34,
 36–37, 39–41, 46, 62, 68, 74,
 84–87, 103–104, 107–108,
 114–115, 119–120, 127, 141
Kimball, Sally 41, 107

King, Dr. Martin Luther, Jr. vii, xv,
 6–10, 55, 78, 81, 94, 106, 123,
 126, 128, 131, 175, 179
Ku Klux Klan xv, 12, 30, 32,
 36–37, 41, 74, 86, 91, 93, 97,
 100, 104, 109, 113, 116, 120,
 127

L

Lang, Pat 92, 99–102 141
Laurence 52–54, 142
Lawson, James, Reverend 11–12
Leonard, Janis 19–20, 26–28
Leonard, Mrs. 19–20, 27–28
"Letter from a Birmingham City
 Jail" 9
Limestone College, Gaffney, South
 Carolina 150
Little Rock, Arkansas 54
Lloyd, Beatrice 142

M

Middleton, Celi Mariah 35
Middleton, Willie, Reverend 108,
 114, 116, 121, 142
Mitchell, Herbert 41, 83, 101,
 103–105, 113, 127, 133, 138,
 142
Mississippi 12, 14, 106, 123, 176
Moncks Corner 40, 42, 54, 80, 82,
 92, 94–95, 99, 115, 117, 118,
 120
Morris Brown College 1, 5, 10
Moultrie, Henry 41, 100, 103–
 104, 121–122, 142
Moultrie, Victoria 145

Movement, The xiv, xvii, 1, 3, 5, 8, 10–11, 28, 44, 51, 106, 108, 123, 143, 172, 176
Myers, Thomas 144

N

National Association for the Advancement of Colored People (NAACP) 29, 41–42, 50, 54, 61–62, 85, 108, 124, 149
Nelson, Ray xvi, xviii, 2–3, 5, 7, 16–17, 19, 24–25, 50 134, 138, 141, 145
nonviolence 9–11, 120

O

On Civil Disobedience xiii
101st Airborne 54
Orangeburg Massacre 144
orientation xvii, 2, 7, 11, 20, 39, 54, 71–72, 85, 90, 109, 151, 179
orientation schedule 153–162

P

Perry, Matthew 61–65
Pineville x, xv–xvi, 29–30, 32–33, 35–36, 39, 41, 44–45, 47, 50–51, 56, 59–60, 67, 69–74, 77, 81, 84, 86–87, 93, 95, 103, 106–107, 110, 112–113, 115, 122, 124, 126–127, 130, 132, 134, 138, 141–149, 151, 168–169, 171, 176

Prioleau, Ishmael, Jr. 70–76, 84–85, 120, 123, 130, 133–134, 138, 142
Prioleau, Reginald 35, 49, 169
Prioleau, Willie Louis 120, 123, 131, 142

R

Ravenell, Maxine 46, 52–53, 74, 94, 96, 98, 121–122, 127, 133, 142
Ravenell, Roger 142
Redeemer Reformed Episcopal Church 41, 80, 87–88, 90, 104–105, 107, 114, 127, 131–132, 168, 171, 179
Rose, Doris 55, 116, 142
Route 66 3
Russellville High School 53
Rustin, Bayard 9

S

Sanders, Carol xvi, 2–3, 5, 15–16, 18, 21–24, 34, 50, 103–104, 107, 112, 119, 132, 138, 141, 179
SCLC xi, xvii, 2–3, 6–8, 10–11, 14, 18–19, 29, 35, 39, 42, 67–68, 71, 85, 108, 118–119, 127, 153–165
SCOPE xvii–xviii, 2–3, 6, 16–17, 24, 50, 61, 71, 93, 121, 130, 175, 179
segregation xvii, 8–9, 21, 86, 131
Selma-to-Montgomery March xiv, xviii, 126

Simmons, Coretta 138, 149, 169, 179
Simmons, George 121, 127, 134–135, 142, 149, 168
Simmons, Lula Mae 40, 44–47, 50, 52–53, 55, 74, 94, 96, 121, 123, 127, 132–133, 138, 142
Simmons, Martha Ann Middleton Prioleau xi, 34, 35, 41, 68, 74, 87, 104–106, 124, 134–135, 142, 149, 167–169, 171, 173
Smalls, Chequetta 138, 149–150
Smalls, Lottie 138, 151–152
Smalls, Ontario 138, 149–150
South Carolina Law Enforcement Division (SLED) 115
Southern Christian Leadership Conference (*see* SCLC)
St. Augustine, Florida 12, 14
St. Stephen High School 54, 168
Student Nonviolent Coordinating Committee (SNCC) xvii, 14
Summer Community Organization and Political Education Project (*see* SCOPE)
Summers, James (Butch) 37, 83, 122–123, 126, 132–133, 138, 142
Sumpter, Gregory 49, 79, 138
Sumpter, Theresa (Cutie) 138, 146, 151
Swinton, Joe 41, 142

T

TenBrink, Julie xvi, xviii, 2–3, 5, 16, 25, 50, 62, 66, 71, 107, 118, 131–132, 138, 141, 179
The Souls of Black Folk 19
Thoreau, Henry David xiii, xv

U

University of California, Berkeley xiv, xviii, 2, 10, 29, 39, 141

V

Vaughn 142
voter registration worker 39, 62, 68

W

Walter 112, 142
Washington, Kenny 41, 94–97, 100, 102, 109, 113, 115, 120, 122–123, 127, 142
Washington, Lucille 138, 146–147
White, Deke (Leon) 55–59, 83, 108, 137, 139, 142, 145
Williams, Deborah 138, 150
Williams, Hosea xvii, 9, 16, 175, 179
Williams, Ike 118

Y

Young, Andrew 71, 151

To order copies of this book visit:

www.sherielabedis.com